HENRIK IBSEN

A Doll's House

Translated from the Norwegian by
MICHAEL MEYER

With commentary and notes by
NICK *and* NON WORRALL

METHUEN DRAMA

Methuen Drama Student Edition

Methuen Drama, an imprint of Bloomsbury Publishing Plc

10 9 8 7 6

This edition first published in Great Britain in 1985 by Methuen London Ltd
Reprinted with corrections 1991 by Methuen Drama
Reissued with a new cover design 1994
Reissued with additional material and a new cover design 2005
Revised edition 2008
Reissued with a new cover design 2009

Methuen Drama,
Bloomsbury Publishing Plc
49–51 Bedford Square
London W1CB 3DP
www.methuendrama.com

A Doll's House first published in this translation in 1965 by Rupert Hart-Davis Ltd,
and subsequently by Eyre Methuen Ltd in 1974
Copyright © Michael Meyer 1965
Commentary and Notes copyright © 1985, 2005, 2008 by Methuen Drama

The right of Michael Meyer to be identified as the translator of this play has been
asserted by him in accordance with the Copyright, Designs and Patents Act 1988

ISBN 978 1 408 10602 0

A CIP catalogue record for this book is available from the British Library

Available in the USA from Bloomsbury Academic & Professional,
175 Fifth Avenue/3rd Floor, New York, NY 10010.
www.BloomsburyAcademicUSA.com

Printed and bound in Great Britain by CPI Group (UK) Ltd, Croydon CR0 4YY

Contents

Photographs (by Donald Cooper) of the 1981/2 Royal Shakespeare Company production directed by Adrian Noble with Cheryl Campbell (Nora), Stephen Moore (Torvald), Bernard Lloyd (Krogstad), Marjorie Bland (Mrs Linde) and John Franklyn-Robbins (Rank) appear on pages iv, xii, xlix, 112–14.

Note: the pages of the play-text are numbered so that they accord with the numbering in *Ibsen Plays: Two* for those working in groups which have both editions.

Nora with (*above*) Mrs Linde and (*below*) Krogstad

Henrik Johan Ibsen: 1828–1906

1828   20 March: born in Norway at Skien, a small town on the
east coast a hundred miles from the capital, Christiania
(now Oslo), the second of five children of Knud Ibsen, a
merchant, and his wife, Marichen.

1834   Family life drastically affected by Knud's financial
difficulties. Henrik's own unhappiness compounded by
hearing rumours that he was not Knud's son. The boy
seems to have believed them despite his strong physical
resemblance to his father.

1835   The family had to move to their small country house at
Vernstoep, the rest of their property having been seized for
payment of debts. It is not certain what kind of education
Henrik received.

1841   Enrolled, aged 13, at a small private school where his
favourite subjects were history and religion. He also learnt
German and Latin as well as drawing.

1843   Left school when family moved to Snipetorp on the out-
skirts of Skien. Knud never regained financial respectability
being ultimately categorized as a 'pauper'.

1844   3 January: apprenticed to an apothecary, Reimann, in small
provincial shipping town of Grimstad. Extremely badly
paid and overworked, with rarely enough to eat, he still
found time to paint, draw caricatures of and compose
lampoons about local citizens, write serious poetry and read
an enormous amount. Although he shared a bedroom with
the apothecary's older sons, he studied at night for
matriculation in the hope that he might be able to go to
university.

1846   9 October: birth of Ibsen's illegitimate son to Else
Jensdatter, one of Reimann's maids.

1848   Year of Revolutions throughout Europe. Ibsen entered
enthusiastically into Republican oratory at various public
meetings.
Summer: visited his family in Skien but there is no record
of his or their response.

1849   January — March: private publication of *Catiline*, a play
in blank verse about the failure of the conspiracy against
Rome led by Catiline. It sold only 45 copies and was not
accepted for performance by any theatre.
September: *In Autumn,* a poem, was first Ibsen work to
be published under the pseudonym, Brynjolf Bjarme in
Christiania Post.

1850   April: terminated his employment and went to visit his
family en route for university at Christiania. He never saw
his parents or brothers again and even stopped writing
letters home '. . . chiefly because I could not be of any
assistance or support to my parents.' (Letter of 1877).
Took lodgings in Christiania and enlisted at a crammer to
prepare for the matriculation exam in August. Consolidated
his links with the Socialist movement through his friendships
with Aasmund Vinje and Theodor Abildgaard. Met
Bjoernstjerne Bjoernson, left-wing politician, intellectual and
playwright, with whom he was to have a lifelong love/hate
relationship.
August: failed his matriculation exam and therefore could
not graduate from university.
26 September: first performance of *The Warrior's Barrow,*
which was in tune with the fashion for romantic
nationalism. Well received.

1851   Became editor of *Samfundsbladet,* handwritten magazine
of the Students' Union, but his interest declined as he
became theatre critic of a new literary and political weekly,
Manden.
7 July: the offices of the radical newspaper *Arbejder
foreningernes,* to which Ibsen also contributed, were
raided by the police. Abildgaard, the editor, and Thrane,
founder of the workers' movement in Norway, were
imprisoned for three years, but Ibsen kept quiet. As
Michael Meyer remarks: 'Ibsen's courage throughout his life
was limited to the written word.'
6 November: offered job as 'dramatic author' at £5 a
month by Ole Bull at the Norwegian Theatre in Bergen
which had been founded in January 1850 as part of a widespread desire to develop a specifically national culture.
During the next six years, Ibsen wrote, directed, designed
sets and costumes and saw to the business and financial
affairs of the theatre.

1852   April: using £50 grant from the government, Ibsen visited theatres in Denmark and Copenhagen to extend his knowledge and experience.
Autumn: *St. John's Night*, a 'fairy tale comedy', performed at the Norwegian Theatre, was an enormous failure.

1855   2 January: *Lady Inger of Oestraat*, historical tragedy written in prose, was a total failure on its premiere at Bergen. By this time, however, Ibsen's financial position was much improved. During this year he first came across the Icelandic Sagas by which he was fascinated.

1856   2 January: *The Feast at Solhaug*, a melodrama about two sisters who are in love with the same man, was greeted with delight by Bergen audiences largely because of the medieval costumes and setting, despite the fact that it is a weak play.
7 January: met Suzannah Thoresen to whom he became engaged within a month.

1857   2 January: *Olaf Liljekrans* performed to open the Bergen season. Peter Blytt noted: '. . . little understood and was not a success; the audience, which had filled the theatre, hugely expectant, left in a cool mood.'
Autumn: left Bergen to become artistic director of the Norwegian Theatre of Christiania, which had been founded in 1852 as an angry reaction by a few extreme patriots against the failure of the Bergen Theatre to live up to its ideals.

1858   June: marriage to Suzannah Thoresen in Bergen.
23 August: with the opening of a new season at the theatre, Ibsen gradually introduced new attitudes and plays.
Produced *The Vikings at Helgeland*, an historical prose tragedy, which enjoyed a limited success. Also directed two Holberg comedies and one Molière during this season, but the staple fare was largely unchanged.

1859   October: local press criticisms of his choice of plays for production were countered by Ibsen.
23 December: birth of Sigurd, the Ibsens' only child.

1860   Audiences seemed to want a diet of light comedy, preferably with music and dancing; Ibsen in despair.

1861   Attacks on Ibsen's conduct of the Norwegian Theatre published in the Christiania press. Rebuked by Theatre Board for lack of effort, Ibsen remained silent but was vigorously defended by Paul Botten Hansen.

1862   May: travelled extensively in Norway on grant from University of Christiania to compile folk songs and tales.

Summer: Norwegian Theatre of Christiania declared bankrupt and forced to close.

December: *Love's Comedy*, a modern verse satire, published.

1863   1 January: became part-time literary adviser to the Danish Christiania Theatre, which rejected *Love's Comedy* largely because of newspaper reviews which had declared it immoral for demonstrating that love and marriage are not necessarily synonymous.

Ibsen was so poor he had to borrow from moneylenders. Government rejected his application for financial support but eventually granted him a travel stipend which was augmented by a collection raised by Bjoernson and other friends.

December: Ibsen was appalled and ashamed that the Norwegian government did not come to the aid of Denmark in resisting Prussia.

1864   17 January: first performance of *The Pretenders*, historical prose tragedy, directed by Ibsen himself at the Christiania Theatre. Received enthusiastically.

5 April: left for Copenhagen, travelling from there to Rome which he eventually reached in mid-June. Remained resident abroad for twenty-seven years. Began writing *Emperor and Galilean*.

1865   14 November: signed a contract with Frederick Hegel, head of Gyldendal publishing firm in Copenhagen.

1866   15 March: publication of *Brand*, a play written to be *read*. It created an immediate sensation, establishing Ibsen's reputation throughout Scandinavia.

April-June: the Storthing (the Norwegian parliament) voted Ibsen grants and an annual stipend.

1867   14 November: publication of *Peer Gynt*, also written to be read; again a success.

1868   October: moved from Rome to Dresden.

1869   18 October: *The League of Youth*, a modern prose comedy, performed at the Christiania Theatre. There was controversy and uproar as progressive personalities were offended by their apparent characterization in the play. One of the characters, chafing against the bonds of marriage, complains to her husband: 'You dressed me up like a doll; you played with me as one plays with a child.' In his review, the Danish critic, Georg Brandes, suggested that such a character might make a good central figure for a later work. October-November: attended the opening of the Suez Canal as Norwegian delegate.

1873 1 January: *Ibsen, the Norwegian Satirist,* a long article written by Edmund Gosse, was the first full assessment of Ibsen in English.

16 October: *Emperor and Galilean,* Ibsen's last historical play, was published and extremely well received. Written on an epic scale, its central theme concerns the search for a religion which would combine Christian ethics with the joy of life.

1874 July-September: to the delight of the general public, Ibsen returned to Norway for the first time in ten years. The students held a torchlight parade in his honour. Ibsen, however, did not feel at ease and returned abroad.

1875 April: the Ibsens moved from Dresden to Munich for the benefit of Sigurd's education and because it was a cheaper place to live.

1876 24 February: premiere of *Peer Gynt,* with Grieg's musical score, at the Christiania Theatre. It was the theatre's most expensive production and proved an outstanding success, although Ibsen disliked the music.

10 April: *The Vikings at Helgeland* performed to acclaim at Munich Hoftheater, the first of Ibsen's plays to be staged outside Scandinavia.

June: as a guest of honour, Ibsen watched the Duke of Saxe-Meiningen's production of *The Pretenders* by which he was greatly impressed.

1877 11 October: publication of *The Pillars of Society,* an immediate and widespread success, particularly in Germany, where it was frequently staged.

1878 The Ibsens returned to Italy to live for one year only.

1879 4 December: publication of *A Doll's House,* a sensational success in Scandinavia and Germany, running through three editions within three months.

21 December: world premiere of *A Doll's House* at the Royal Theatre, Copenhagen. The family moved back to Munich.

1880 Autumn: the Ibsens return to Italy, this time for five years. *The Pillars of Society,* translated by William Archer, was the first Ibsen play to be performed in England — a single matinée in London.

1881   December: publication of *Ghosts* immediately provoked great controversy. Booksellers returned copies to the publisher; no Scandinavian theatre would accept the play for production. Sales of other Ibsen plays were adversely affected.

1882   May: first performance of *Ghosts* took place in Chicago, in Norwegian before an audience of Scandinavian immigrants.

2 June: first performance in English of *A Doll's House* (in a very free adaptation) in Milwaukee, U.S.A.

28 November: publication of *An Enemy of the People* met with mixed reception but theatres were keen to produce it.

1883   28 August: first European performance of *Ghosts* took place in Helsingborg, Sweden. The production, directed by Lindberg, toured various Scandinavian cities, playing to full, enthusiastic houses.

1884   3 March: an extremely free adaptation of *A Doll's House* performed in London.

11 November: general bewilderment amongst critics and public alike on the publication of *The Wild Duck*.

1885   June-September: Ibsen made only his second visit to Norway in twenty years.

October: the Ibsens moved from Rome to Munich.

1886   22 November: invited to attend the very successful, private Saxe-Meiningen production of *Ghosts,* but the Censor would not allow a public performance.

23 November: publication of *Rosmersholm* accorded a hostile press. The play was rejected by theatres.

1888   28 November: *The Lady From The Sea* was published.

December: first English edition of Ibsen, containing *The Pillars of Society, A Doll's House* and *An Enemy of the People,* sold extremely well.

1889   7 June: *A Doll's House,* translated by William Archer, presented at Kingsway Theatre, London, with Janet Achurch as Nora. Newspaper reviews were generally unfavourable — 'It would be a misfortune were such a morbid and unwholesome play to gain the favour of the public' (*Standard*) — but such as Harley Granville Barker, Bernard Shaw and W.B. Yeats reacted quite differently, realising that they were witnessing 'an epoch-making venture in the higher drama' (Barker: *The Coming of Ibsen*).

This production toured Australia, New Zealand, Egypt, India and America.

21 July: Ibsen met 18 year old Emilie Bardach at Gossensass. He became passionately attached to her and she to him but she left Gossensass on 27 September. In the following years Ibsen became infatuated with a series of young women.

1890 29 May: *Ghosts* staged by André Antoine in Paris.

18 July: G.B. Shaw delivered a lecture on Ibsen, later published as *The Quintessence of Ibsenism*, to the Fabian Society in London, provoking controversy about Ibsen's 'socialism'. The high level of interest in Ibsen's work in England encouraged William Heinemann to offer him a publication contract.

16 December: *Hedda Gabler* was published and received most unfavourably, as it was almost everywhere when first performed.

1891 13 March: London première of *Ghosts* presented by Jacob T. Grein for the Independent Theatre Society. The majority of critics were outraged by the play's subject matter: 'As foul and filthy a concoction as has ever been allowed to disgrace the boards of an English theatre' (*Era*). The uproar ensured that Ibsen became a household name. Archer compiled a collection of the reactions to Grein's production which was published as *Ghosts and Gibberings* in the *Pall Mall Gazette*.

July: Ibsen returned to live in Norway.

1892 12 December: publication of *The Master Builder* received a better press than its recent predecessors although there was still some bewilderment.

16 December: Lugné-Poë presented *The Lady from the Sea* in Paris, the first of his several Ibsen productions.

1894 11 December: an almost unanimously favourable reception greeted *Little Eyolf*'s publication. The play proved to be an immense commercial success.

1895 27 June: largely because he could not speak English, Ibsen refused Archer's invitation to visit London.

1896 15 December: publication of *John Gabriel Borkman*. Demand exceeded supply.

1899 19 February: Moscow Art Theatre staged their first Ibsen production, *Hedda Gabler* with Stanislavsky as Loevborg.

22 December: *When We Dead Awaken* published and

respectfully received.

1900 Suffered his first stroke. Left partly paralysed.
1901 A second stroke left him unable to write or walk.
1906 23 May: Ibsen died aged 78.

Nora and Torvald

Plot

Act One

It is Christmas Eve in the comfortably furnished living-room of the Helmers' apartment. Nora Helmer enters, dressed against the cold, laden with parcels, leaving a porter at the door carrying a Christmas tree, which she instructs the maid to hide. She gives the porter a generous tip. She nibbles delightedly at some macaroons she has bought and then hurriedly hides them when her husband, Torvald Helmer, appears from his study. It becomes evident that he has been appointed manager of a bank after a period of insecurity and Nora is keen to spend more now that they no longer have to economise. Helmer, however, points out that his new salary does not start until April and teasingly asks how she would cope with debts if he were to die unexpectedly. He does then give her extra money to spend on presents and asks what she would like for Christmas. Nora promptly asks for money. In a succession of affectionate speeches, Helmer rebukes her for squandering money, hinting that she inherits this trait from her father. In answer to his inquiry as to whether she has bought any sweets or cakes in town, she lies. Helmer is delighted that his appointment means that they will be comfortable and secure; Nora will not have to spend time laboriously making the Christmas decorations which he believes she spent hours doing the previous year.

The maid announces two visitors; an unknown woman, who is shown into the living-room, and Dr. Rank, who is shown into Helmer's study through an off-stage door. Helmer goes out to speak to his friend while Nora greets the stranger whom, after a momentary blankness, she recognises as Christine Linde, an old school friend whom she has not seen for nearly ten years. Through their conversation, it is revealed that Mrs. Linde had married a man she did not love to give security to her bedridden mother and two younger brothers. Her husband had died bankrupt three years previously leaving Mrs Linde with nothing. Her mother has now died and her brothers have found jobs, so after three years of extremely hard work and poverty, she is free to make her own life. On hearing of Helmer's appointment, she becomes hopeful of finding employment at the bank. Nora expresses sympathy over her friend's difficult life and, to prove that she too can be strong and helpful, proudly asserts her own contribution to solving the problems of her own family situation. Soon after they had married, Helmer became ill. The doctor insisted that it was necessary for him to rest and stay in a warm country for a year or he would die. They had no money; Helmer would not run up debts. Nora borrowed the money secretly, telling her husband that it came from her father. Over the years she has managed to pay the quarterly instalments and interest. Now Nora anticipates that their new wealth will solve her problems of paying off the debt. She has not told Helmer; it would hurt his pride.

Krogstad, who works at the bank, is announced. His appearance startles Mrs. Linde. Nora speaks tensely and secretively to him but Krogstad has called to see Helmer on bank business. Dr. Rank joins the women when Krogstad enters Helmer's study. Rank forcefully expresses his low opinion of Krogstad's moral character. Nora laughingly offers him a macaroon, pretending that she has been given them by Mrs. Linde.

Having sent Krogstad on his way, Helmer returns. Nora immediately asks him to give her friend employment. He agrees. Nora reminds Mrs. Linde and Dr. Rank that they are expected back in the evening, and as they and Helmer leave, the nurse, Anne-Marie, brings the three children in. They have been sledging. Sending the nurse to have some coffee, Nora chatters to, and plays hide-and-seek with, her children. While she is playing, Krogstad appears, unannounced. Startled, Nora sends the children off to the nurse so that she may speak privately with him. In their conversation, Krogstad, having established that he once knew Mrs. Linde, asks Nora to use her influence with her husband to prevent Helmer dismissing him from his subordinate position in the bank. When Nora is unwilling, Krogstad threatens to reveal to Helmer that it is he who has been receiving Nora's repayments, and hints at blackmail. He is prepared to do anything to safeguard his position as it ensures his current respectability after a period of social disgrace. Nora's vehement insistence that he may do his worst, draws Krogstad into explaining fully the effects upon Helmer of Nora's actions. It becomes clear that he knows that, in order to borrow the money from Krogstad in the first place, Nora had forged her father's signature as security for the debt and had carelessly dated the document three days after her father's death. Nora refuses to believe that the law would find her guilty of any crime since her action was determined by the best of motives, love. Krogstad leaves, threatening that he will destroy her happy family life if he loses his job.

Trying to dismiss Krogstad's threats, Nora throws herself energetically into decorating the Christmas tree. Helmer enters enquiring what Krogstad had wanted. When Nora asks exactly what he had done to merit disgrace, Helmer condemns Krogstad not just for committing the original crime of forgery but for failing to admit it and accept his punishment. Such dishonesty infects a person's family, particularly the children. Nora applies what Helmer says about Krogstad to herself. When he goes into his study, she will not allow the children to come in to her. She is superstitiously fearful that she will infect them with her own corruption.

Act Two

The Christmas tree is stripped of its decorations and the candles are burnt out. Nora is alone, worrying about whether a letter of denunciation will arrive from Krogstad. The nurse brings her a box of fancy-dress clothes to look at. In their conversation it becomes clear that Nora has decided to have as little contact as possible with her children, comforting herself with the thought that the nurse will always look after them.

Mrs. Linde arrives and helps Nora repair the costume of a Neapolitan fisher-girl which Helmer wants his wife to wear to dance the tarantella at a party to be held in the upstairs flat that evening. Nora explains that Dr. Rank is suffering from spinal tuberculosis, inherited as a result of his father's debauchery. She refutes Mrs. Linde's suspicions about the source of the loan. Hearing Helmer returning, she hustles Mrs. Linde and her sewing into the next room on the pretext of hiding the fancy-dress costume from him. She then makes one last attempt to persuade Helmer not to dismiss Krogstad. Helmer refuses, revealing his anxiety that Krogstad may, by presuming upon his old school friendship with Helmer, become a personal embarrassment. Nora cannot believe such petty reasoning. This stings Helmer into sending off the letter of dismissal instantly. To calm Nora's ensuing panic, Helmer makes a general claim that he would always shoulder the burden of her problems if the need arose. As he goes into his study, Nora's desperate anxiety becomes evident. Her self-questioning as to what course to take is interrupted by the arrival of Dr. Rank.

Rank has chosen this moment to explain to Nora that he
expects to die within a month. He arranges to leave Nora a visiting
card with a black cross on it when he knows that the final stage of
his illness has been reached. In the fading light Nora impulsively
decides to flirt with Rank, tantalising him with the idea of her
wearing silk stockings. She toys with the idea of seeking his help
but as she is building up to the point of asking him for money, he
declares that his visits to the Helmers are on her account. His
confession of love renders her request for money impossible as
it would place their relationship on an openly explicit level. She
chides Rank for spoiling the game she has enjoyed playing; he
has provided the sense of fun and amusement lacking in her
relationship with Helmer.

The maid enters with Krogstad's visiting card. Nora sends Rank
into Helmer's study with the request that he keep Helmer engaged
on the pretext that a new dress has been delivered which she wishes
to keep secret from her husband. Krogstad has not come to expose
her publicly but to blackmail Helmer. He will keep Nora's IOU to
pressurise Helmer into giving him a new job as assistant manager
at the bank. He warns Nora against desperate acts such as suicide,
since Helmer would still suffer from the ensuing scandal. As he
leaves, Krogstad drops a letter in which he reveals all to Helmer
in the letter box.

Mrs. Linde re-enters to find Nora looking as if she has seen a
ghost. When Nora points out the letter to her, she realises that it
was Krogstad who lent Nora the money. She leaves to try to use
her influence with him while Nora tries to prevent Helmer from
opening the letter. This she does by persuading him that the most
important thing is for him to help her practise the tarantella.
Firstly to Helmer's and then to Rank's piano accompaniment,
the rehearsal becomes frantic on Nora's part as she keeps dancing
desperately until Mrs. Linde returns. To humour Nora, and at her
insistence, Helmer promises not to deal with any business,
including the opening of letters, until after the party is over.
Delaying Mrs. Linde from following the men into dinner, Nora is
told that Krogstad has left town and will not return until the
following evening. Left alone Nora reveals that this means she has
only thirty-one hours to live. When her husband appears asking for
his songbird, she runs to him with open arms.

Act Three
It is late at night; dance music can be heard from the floor above.

Alone, Mrs. Linde sits waiting anxiously. The person she is waiting for arrives. It is Krogstad. She explains that she had to jilt him in the past out of duty to her family simply because he had so little money. She asks him if he would now accept her back since they both need each other. He is delighted, and when he realises Mrs. Linde knows of the steps he has taken against the Helmers, he suggests asking for his letter back. She, however, insists that Helmer must know the truth if he and Nora are to achieve a 'full understanding' (p.84). Krogstad leaves. Mrs. Linde is overjoyed at having a second chance of happiness.

Helmer leads Nora in almost forcibly. She is most reluctant to leave the party but he has insisted that they come home. Mrs. Linde explains away her presence, saying how much she wanted to see Nora in her costume. Helmer is only too willing to show off his wife's beauty. When he leaves to fetch more candles, Mrs. Linde hurriedly tells Nora she has nothing to fear from Krogstad but that she must tell Helmer the truth or else the letter will. Nora replies enigmatically that she now knows what she must do. Mrs. Linde rapidly takes her leave, to Helmer's obvious relief. His desires roused by Nora's dancing, he has dragged her home to make love to her. She rejects his advances; his appeal to his conjugal rights is cut off by a knock at the door. Dr. Rank has also left the party and dropped by on his way home to borrow a cigar. Nora understands the significance of his parting words and of the two visiting cards with black crosses which he drops into the letter box. Nora's explanation distracts Helmer from desiring her and she then firmly asks him to read his letters. He goes into his study to do so.

Left alone, Nora wraps herself in Helmer's black cloak, throws a shawl over her head and is about to run off, apparently to drown herself, when Helmer appears holding the open letter. He demands an explanation but, without allowing her to give one, accuses her of ruining his life and claims she has no sense of religion, morality · or duty. To avoid a scandal he will do whatever Krogstad wants. Nora's assertion that he will be free when she has committed suicide merely angers him for he would still have to face the scandal that Krogstad could create. He insists that they must keep up the appearance of man and wife, but the children will not be in her care and his love for her is gone.

A letter arrives for Nora which Helmer opens. It contains the IOU returned by Krogstad. Helmer now reverses his attitude towards Nora, stating that he knows she only acted out of love for him and that only her inexperience caused her to choose the wrong

means. As Nora takes off her fancy-dress in the next room, he
continues to talk about her as a helpless little creature whom he
will look after.

Nora re-appears in her everyday clothes and insists on discussing
their marriage. Pointing out that this is their first serious talk
together in eight years, Nora explains to Helmer how she has been
treated, first by her father and then by her husband, the two who
have professed to love her more than anyone in the world. She now
understands that it has all been a game, where she has been a doll
who has been played with. Helmer agrees there may be a little
truth in what she says but that the time has now come for him to
educate her instead of play with her. Nora, however, insists that
she must educate herself. She must find out independently the
truth about herself and about life. To this end she is leaving
Helmer. Rejecting his claim that her duties are to her husband and
children, Nora steadfastly vows that her first duty is to herself as a
human being. No longer prepared to accept the dictates of religion
or the morality of a society whose laws would have condemned
her, she is determined to establish her own identity and
philosophy. Her husband destroyed her faith in miracles when he
lacked the strength to stand up to Krogstad's threats or shoulder
his wife's blame. To compound this weakness, when the danger was
past, he wanted to behave as if nothing had happened. Nora no
longer loves him because he is not the man she thought he was.
Collecting only a small travelling bag, and after returning Helmer's
wedding ring and making him return hers, she leaves, forbidding
him even to write to her. Helmer collapses distressed into a chair.
His last hope that she might change her mind is shattered by the
sound of Nora slamming the street door.

Commentary

The historical situation

The sparsely populated country in which Ibsen grew up was a predominantly agrarian society highly dependent on maritime trade. Politically subjugated, by annexation to Denmark until 1814 and then by enforced union with Sweden, Norway nevertheless had not been 'colonised' and was more democratic than most other European countries, with nearly half the adult population being entitled to the vote. There was virtually no indigenous aristocracy, as a result of the ravages of the Black Death in the Middle Ages, and in 1821 the Norwegian Parliament, the Storthing, abolished all orders of nobility.

A period of rapid industrialization after 1884 affected life in the urban areas, although Norwegian society was noticeably sluggish in its assimilation of new inventions and the material comforts which flowed from them. The gap between the lifestyle of town and country became gradually more pronounced, and this added to the problems caused by long-established language divisions. The prolonged union with Denmark had resulted in the use of two distinct languages: 'riksmal', a form of written Danish incorporating a substantial Norwegian vocabulary, which was the official language of the church and state, and 'landsmal', spoken Norwegian dialects used in everyday life, especially in the countryside. Ibsen wrote his plays in 'riksmal' for a predominantly middle-class urban audience.

Ibsen and nineteenth-century Norwegian theatre

Norway remained culturally dependent on Denmark long after 1814. This is particularly evident in the history and evolution of Norway's theatre, which has no distinct and lengthy tradition although theatrical performances can be traced back to the Middle Ages. The first real steps towards an independent tradition came with the establishment of permanent theatre buildings and professional acting companies during the nineteenth-century.

During the late eighteenth century, amateur dramatic societies abounded, each consisting of a few hundred members, every one of whom was prepared to participate actively in one or more of the productions. The oldest was founded in the capital, Christiania (now Oslo), in 1780. These companies enthusiastically presented a type of repertory culled from the Royal Theatre in Copenhagen, featuring a varied programme of contemporary vaudevilles, bourgeois dramas and light comedies. Through the energy and commitment of these amateur groups, many Norwegian towns acquired technical equipment in permanent playhouses, the first of which was opened in Bergen on 3 December 1800.

The Christiania Theatre was opened in January 1827 with a permanent company of local actors, but adverse criticism of their standards forced them to import Danish players. This was a recurring problem for many years. Audiences were reluctant to wait for the native talent to acquire the professional expertise they had come to expect from visiting companies. The enormous number of plays presented – for example, sixty different productions in the first Christiania season – were by French, Danish and German writers; when Ibsen's *Catiline* appeared in 1850, it was the first Norwegian drama to be published for seven years.

The tide of optimistic nationalist feeling that was rising during the middle years of the nineteenth century brought important changes in the Norwegian theatre. On 2 January 1850 Ole Bull launched the first professional theatre, in Bergen, with a production of Holberg's *The Weathercock*. It was here that Ibsen acquired his initial practical experience during a period of transition as the theatre moved towards a more naturalistic mode of performance and away from the grandeur of romanticism.

By today's standards, they had relatively few rehearsals. There were recognized rules and conventions with regard to stage positioning, within which the individual actor was pretty much left to prepare his own role. It was usual to divide directorial responsibilities between two people: thus Ibsen was assigned stage direction – that is, all matters concerning the *appearance* of the play on stage – whereas someone else was in charge of role direction, which included analysing the play and instructing the actor so that he fully understood his part.

The stage conditions at the Bergen theatre when Ibsen went to work there were 'some fifty years behind the times and resembled those commonly to be found on the Continent and in England during the eighteenth century' (Meyer, *Ibsen*, Penguin p.125). The sets were not solidly constructed to look realistic but consisted of a painted backcloth with a series of side-wings and overhead borders. When the scene needed to be changed, the wings, mounted on wheels, were cranked along grooves in the floor and the backcloth would be rolled up and another lowered as appropriate. The stage was lit by chandeliers above, with footlights ranged along the front, while lamps were arranged behind the various wings to cast light from the sides. The lighting was by candles or petroleum lamps, which meant that the stage and sets were often affected by smoke, wax and oil-stains. Furniture and properties including doors, windows, mirrors and utensils were painted on the wings and backcloth, a technique still sometimes used in British Christmas pantomimes.

A significant contribution to the new trends in Norwegian drama and theatre was made by Bjoernstjerne Bjoernson, a popular leader, journalist, novelist, director and theatre manager as well as dramatist. In 1865 his overwhelmingly successful problem play, *The Newly Wedded Couple*, was staged simultaneously in Copenhagen, Stockholm and Christiania. For more than ten years Bjoernson had been demanding a drama more in tune with contemporary life. In 1885 in an article in the newspaper, *Morgenbladet*, he stated:

> People are delving more deeply into human nature from every angle, in science as well as in art. We investigate each minutest trait, we dissect and analyse . . . And in art this current of naturalism reveals itself in theatrical terms in a strong demand for individualisation.

The enemies were romanticism and the French 'well-made play' with its over-complex plot structure and implausible psychology. The audiences, however, were reluctant to change their accustomed diet.

Where romanticism generally depicted unreal situations involving royal personages in heroic tragedies written in rhymed verse, and encouraged highly theatrical declamatory acting styles, the 'well-made play' was superficially more like real life. The characters were more recognisable as everyday types and the subject matter at least appeared to have more in common with the lives of the audience. The actors, however, had no need to alter their style drastically since these plays, written by the followers of the French dramatist Eugène Scribe (1791-1861), had no depth of psychological characterisation and depended on over-elaborate intricacies of plot to retain the audience's interest. The costumes might be contemporary, the dialogue in prose but these playwrights did not attempt to create individualised characters, relying instead upon a permutation of stock types whom actors and audience immediately recognised and to whom they could make a predictable response. Characterisation had to serve — and frequently was subservient to — the requirements of often implausible plots using theatrically exciting 'trick' effects. There was no serious purpose informing the work of such playwrights, who saw their roles as those of showman and entertainer. Bjoernson sought to change this stage of affairs, but his plays were weakened by his allegiance to the happy ending, which undercut the realistic impulse of his dramas.

The première of *A Doll's House* on 21 December 1879 at the Royal Theatre, Copenhagen, burst upon the contemporary scene because of the radical nature of its subject matter. For the first time audiences were given no easy solutions to a contemporary problem. Helmer, for all his faults, is a loving husband; Nora has recognisable weaknesses as well as strengths. The final curtain is not, in fact, final; the audience are left to contemplate the full effects and likely outcome of Nora's act of rebellion and self-assertion. The style of the production, however, although largely naturalistic in its detailed presentation of an environment, retained a symmetrical arrangement of furniture along the walls, leaving an open, uncluttered playing area. There had only been two blocking rehearsals and eight further rehearsals before the one dress rehearsal. Theatrical traditions die hard.

However, the work of pioneers such as Ludwig Josephson, active during the 1880s at the Christiania Theatre and at the New Theatre in Stockholm, and August Lindberg, whose production of *The Wild Duck* in 1885 'anticipated in almost every respect the naturalism which André Antoine was to introduce five years later at his Théâtre Libre in Paris' (Meyer, p.568), rapidly hastened the demise of the old romanticism, ushering in the new era of stage presentation which could cope with the demands of the new playwrights.

Ibsen had experimented with various dramatic forms and conventions before writing *A Doll's House. The Warrior's Barrow* (1850) was an attempt to fit into the fashion for romantic nationalist drama, and *The Feast at Solhaug* (1856) owed its success to a taste for medievalism. In 1852, whilst on a visit to Copenhagen to study theatrical practice, Ibsen had come across a short treatise by the German scholar Hermann Hettner, entitled

Das Moderne Drama, which advocated that historical plays should be written so as to be psychologically relevant to modern times. Hettner also insisted upon the inappropriateness to serious drama of techniques associated with the 'well-made play'. In serious drama conflict and development of character must hold pride of place. Gradually Ibsen's writing began to reflect his belief in the principles outlined by Hettner. Despite the good reception accorded the historical prose tragedies, *The Vikings at Helgeland* (1857) and *The Pretenders* (1863), Ibsen grew increasingly despondent as it became obvious to him that his native audiences were not going to prove sympathetic to the intrinsically serious impulse behind his writing. By 1864, having endured a series of criticisms in the press of his choice of repertoire for the Norwegian Theatre in Christiania, Ibsen was in despair. He had proved incapable of introducing the reforms he knew were necessary, and his own writing had dried up. His voluntary exile from Norway signalled a conscious break with the live theatre. *Brand* (1865) and *Peer Gynt* (1867) were written to be read and were only staged at a much later date. Nevertheless it is important to note that the poetry they contain and the themes they deal with remain permanent aspects of Ibsen's dramatic concerns even in his prose plays. Although Ibsen spent eight years writing *Emperor and Galilean* (1873), which he later termed his masterpiece, posterity has ignored this, his last historical play. In 1877, as if out of the blue, he wrote *Pillars of Society*, the first successful treatment of a modern topical theme.

In the previous year, the Duke of Saxe-Meiningen had produced *The Pretenders* at his private theatre. Ibsen's move to Munich in 1875 meant he became known in German theatrical circles. He had been delighted by the Meiningen production, which he attended as the Duke's guest. This visit introduced the playwright to a company imbued with the idea of ensemble acting where characterisation was expected to be intelligent and perceptive and where crowds were individualised and properly rehearsed. Sets were designed as an integral part of the play's interpretation, not merely as decor. Ibsen was no longer isolated from these new theatrical developments, which in turn reflected changing attitudes towards society and the role of the theatre. Released from the stultifying provincialism and protestantism of his native land, he was now in an environment in tune with his own aims and intentions. From this point on the direction of his artistic development was assured.

Ibsen's naturalism

Structure

Deriving from concepts outlined in the *Poetics* of Aristotle
(384-322BC), a play which has a small number of characters and
unchanging scene, which takes place over a short period of time,
and which is unified by a single plot, is said to follow the classical
unities. In *A Doll's House* Ibsen has used only five main characters
and a single location (all events take place in the Helmers' apartment). The events in the play span about sixty hours (true classical
unity would demand twenty-four). Such concentration, heightened
by the reduction of the customary five acts to three, creates a
realistic framework, places emphasis on psychology rather than
action and intensifies the force of the drama.

Unlike classical Greek drama, *A Doll's House* has two strands to
the plot, the main one involving Nora, Helmer and Krogstad and
the sub-plot concerning Mrs. Linde and Krogstad. While the two
plots are linked through a series of parallels, the sub-plot distracts
attention from the main plot but is not in itself satisfactory.
Neither Mrs. Linde nor Krogstad are sufficiently well-rounded
characters to be entirely convincing. This signifies a possible
weakness in Ibsen's mastery of his craft which may be excused
given that *A Doll's House* was only his second real attempt at a
modern 'social' drama.

Within the structure of the play, Ibsen has made extensive use
of the device of parallel situation to illuminate the central
predicament of Nora. In the case of Mrs. Linde, for example, Ibsen
establishes a sharp contrast with Nora on her first appearance, a
contrast which Nora herself strives to lessen in her confiding to
the other woman of hardships she has had to overcome. As well as
fulfilling the useful role of confidante to Nora, Mrs. Linde's greater
experience and steadier personality throw Nora's frenzied girlishness
into greater relief. As the play unravels, it is Mrs. Linde who is
responsible for Helmer's discovery of the truth, when it could have
been hidden. Where Mrs. Linde gains security through her liaison
with Krogstad, Nora leaves to face an alien world in which she
must earn her living as well as her independence. Just as Mrs. Linde
is fleeing from the cold emptiness of the world outside, Nora is
preparing to exile herself.

Krogstad in his crime, Dr. Rank in his hereditary disease and
Anne-Marie in her giving up of her illegitimate child, all likewise
serve to amplify Nora's motivation and attitudes. Many further

parallels are drawn between other pairs of characters, for example Krogstad and Helmer. In a play which stresses the danger of avoiding the truth, skilful use of this technique enables the playwright to delineate character by implication and suggestion rather than by direct statement.

As the play progresses an increasing number of facets of 'the truth' are disclosed by hints and deliberate revelations. In this way, in a manner akin to the Greek dramatist Euripides (484-406BC), Ibsen uses what is often referred to as the 'retrospective' method of situation and character delineation. He prefers to begin his tragedy just *before* the catastrophe and to use the dialogue to unravel the preceding events *in retrospect* instead of presenting the actual events on the stage. The influence of the past on the present and the future is carefully explored. The action is concentrated into a very small space of time and the sins of the past are contrasted violently with the calm and comfort of the present, which are swiftly destroyed as retribution approaches. It also makes for a more convincingly realistic depiction of character. For example, Nora's playful extravagance which is carefully established in the opening scene as her dominant trait is gradually demonstrated to be a mask she employs as and when she sees fit. As her secret is slowly revealed, the audience discover the true complexity of her nature. In the manner of real life Ibsen's characters show different aspects of their thought and attitudes in varying situations. Although the characterisation of Mrs. Linde and Krogstad demonstrates some of the difficulties inherent in this technique — the lateness and rapidity of the revelations about their past crucially affect their credibility — *A Doll's House* shows a remarkable sophistication with regard to technique so early in Ibsen's career.

Well versed in the plot devices of the Scribean 'well-made play', where coincidence and revelations of a character's past are used to heighten the audience's anticipation and to resolve the complications of an elaborately complex story line, Ibsen quite deliberately uses these same techniques but to very different effect. The audience is led by a series of hints and ironies to suppose that Nora's dilemma will be happily resolved. We initially anticipate, with Nora, that Helmer will perform the 'miracle' she expects. As this becomes less likely, Mrs. Linde appears to be the character who will provide a happy ending through her influence on Krogstad. Instead she chooses to advise him to allow Helmer to discover the truth. Even in the final act, Krogstad's return of the

IOU and Helmer's desire to revert to the status quo signal the end
of Nora's predicament. This constant reversal of the audience's
expectations forces us to appreciate the true seriousness of the
theme of the play. Ibsen has no easy, comforting solutions to offer;
the conventional hopes and attitudes which inform the 'well-made
play' are shown by implication to be inadequate. Part of the
playwright's intention is to demonstrate the essential shallowness
of the popular plays which used platitudes to hide from the tragic
seriousness of the human condition.

Ibsen uses the stock types and situations familiar to his audience.
Hence there are strong hints that the relationships between Nora,
Helmer and Rank amount to the usual eternal triangle, leading the
audience to suppose that Nora has earned her money, as Mrs. Linde
suspects and as Nora encourages her to believe, through a sexual
liaison with Rank. Just as Krogstad is the 'stage villain' so Mrs.
Linde is 'the woman with a past' but his villainy is mitigated by his
genuine despair at being deserted by her and his desire for social
acceptability, just as her 'past' turns out to be full of dutiful,
conventionally praiseworthy acts instead of the 'dark deeds' we
might have expected. The only obvious device inherited from the
'well-made play' which Ibsen does not turn on its head is the
leaving of the unopened letter in the letter box to heighten
suspense. As Allardyce Nicoll observes, Ibsen 'has learned how to
modify the Scribe formula so as to retain the thrillingly effective
and at the same time to hide the presence of the machinery'
(*World Drama*, Harrap, p.536).

Language

Reviewing the world première of *A Doll's House* at the Royal
Theatre, Copenhagen on 21 December 1879, the Danish playwright
and critic, Erik Boegh wrote:

> It is beyond memory since a play so simple in its action and so
> everyday in its dress made such an impression of artistic mastery
> . . . Not a single declamatory phrase, no high dramatics, no drop
> of blood, not even a tear; never for a moment was the dagger of
> tragedy raised . . . Every needless line is cut, every exchange
> carries the action a step forward, there is not a superfluous
> effect in the whole play . . .

Boegh was obviously impressed by Ibsen's ability to write such an
effective play in contrast to the bombastic melodrama to which
nineteenth-century theatregoers had become accustomed. There

are in fact occasions, most noticeably in Krogstad's words to Nora about the physical effects of suicide by drowning, when Ibsen has deliberate recourse to the very language Boegh praises him for avoiding. As the play proceeds Nora learns the essential impracticality of the romantic posturing embodied in such language. Although frightened she is not deterred by Krogstad's warning – 'Under the ice? Down in the cold, black water? And then, in the spring, to float up again, ugly, unrecognizable, hairless?' (p.73) – but finds her noble intention is regarded as a melodramatic embarrassment by Helmer (p.94). The inappropriateness of such an action is prefigured by the language used by Krogstad, which seems so out of place amidst dialogue designed to sound like that of everyday speech. The seven monologues given to Nora may seem an exception to the overall effect of ordinariness but in fact they are simply broken repetitive utterances which inform us of Nora's increasingly intense inner torment. They are not soliloquies in the normal sense of that word.

Ibsen creates for each character a habit of speech appropriate to his or her own class and personality which is accurately reflected in Michael Meyer's translation. Each one speaks naturally but with a distinctly different voice. Characteristics of Nora's speech are genteel exclamatory expressions such as 'Pooh' or diminutive expressions such as 'Just a tiny bit'. She tends to accumulate short phrases within a series of questions and exclamations: 'Oh, how splendid! We'll have to celebrate! But take off your coat. You're not cold, are you? There!' (p.29). She alternates wheedling with assertiveness – 'If you really want to give me something, you could – you could –' (p.26) and 'Them? Who cares about them? They're strangers' (p.25) – in a way that reflects her lively and excitable nature. When she decides to leave Helmer, her dawning self-awareness is signalled by her use of simply formed declarative sentences: 'I have another duty which is equally sacred' (p.100) and 'Millions of women have done it' (p.102).

Helmer's paternalism and sense of his own importance are reinforced by his distinctive speech. His use of endearments such as 'skylark' and 'squirrel' define his attitude towards his wife. His playful friendliness is often insulting – 'Has my little squanderbird been overspending again?' (p.24) – and his frequently lecturing tone helps to establish his own view of himself in the minds of the audience.

Krogstad's manner of speech shows his legal training in sequences of questions, most noticeably in his enquiries about Mrs.

Linde (p.44-5). The ironically humble fashion in which he speaks of himself, 'Will you be so good as to see that I keep my humble position at the bank?' (p.45), indicates a degree of self-contempt but also seems to blame others for his low status in society. He can be threatening and openly disrespectful, using his skill with words to try to frighten Nora (p.73).

Mrs. Linde and Dr. Rank have almost directly opposite modes of speech. Where he is usually guarded, preferring, as a man of sophistication and breeding, to speak indirectly, using ready-made figures of speech 'With death on my hands?', 'I've been going through the books of this poor body of mine and I find I am bankrupt', 'Laughter's all the damned thing's fit for' (p.65), Mrs. Linde speaks directly to the point but often sounds bitter and cold. Her words reveal a collected, resolved mind certain of its own opinions. She uses ready-made phrases, like Dr. Rank, but without any hint of indirectness. She means what she says whereas he uses words to conceal his real meaning. It is appropriate that it is Mrs. Linde who insists that 'There must be an end of all these shiftings and evasions' (p.84).

Staging

The naturalism identified by Boegh highlights dramatic and theatrical differences between *A Doll's House* and Ibsen's earlier plays. Rebelling against both the heightened romanticism of melodrama and the mechanical complexity of popular light comedies, Ibsen used all his knowledge of the theatrical devices available to a playwright to create a world that was instantly recognisable to his predominantly middle-class audience. As the curtain rises on the set for *A Doll's House* we are looking through the 'fourth wall' into a typical, comfortable, bourgeois drawing-room. Ibsen's careful description delineates exactly how doors and furniture should be positioned. Although at first sight it may seem merely a re-creation of any such room, closer analysis of the play reveals just how integral to the full design and impact of the play is the setting. The realistic details of the opening stage direction are used to lead the audience into a close identification with the characters who inhabit this room which seems so familiar. However Nora, whose cosy environment has been created to suit her husband's tastes, seems, because of her constantly emphasised restlessness, trapped within it. She rarely settles but paces the floor as if in the confines of a cage. It is noticeable that whenever she feels threatened she retreats to the stove, whose warmth seems to

represent the security she so urgently craves. For example, both
Nora at the entry of Mrs. Linde (p.29) and Helmer (p.52) when he
returns from business, have established the stove as the
conventional source of heat but in Nora's actions after Krogstad's
exit in Act One this is extended to include emotional as well as
physical warmth: she 'nods indifferently as she closes the hall door
behind him. Then she walks across the room and sees to the stove'
(p.38). Similarly after Dr. Rank has declared his love for her, she
'goes over to the stove' saying: 'Oh, dear, Dr. Rank, this was really
horrid of you' (p.68). Thus Ibsen uses an apparently naturalistic
method to establish clearly the emotional life of his characters.

Similarly stage properties are used to show most pointedly the
agony of a character's dilemma. When Nora enters at the beginning
of the play, she is bringing home a Christmas tree, the symbol of a
festival concentrating upon renewal of life and family happiness.
The tree is seen only fleetingly but for long enough to establish
both the time of year and Nora's involvement in ensuring her
family's well-being. In an attempt to rid herself of the fears called
up by Krogstad's threatening visit, she calls for the maid to place
the tree in the middle of the room, the focal position in theatrical
terms. Here it stands representing family security and happiness as
Nora tries in vain to concentrate upon its decoration and blot out
her anxieties. Hence before a word is spoken in Act Two, Nora's
failure to allay her fears is already implicitly established by the fate
of the Christmas tree which now stands 'In the corner by the
piano . . . stripped and dishevelled, its candles burned to their
sockets' (p.55).

To look closely at the treatment of a superficially minor
property such as the macaroons is to reveal more of this aspect of
Ibsen's art. When Nora at the beginning of Act One secretly eats a
couple of these small sweet biscuits before concealing the bag from
her husband, Ibsen establishes in a moment and most economically
that Nora has a childish capacity to deceive and delight in secret
rebelliousness and that her husband has a parent's authority over
her. The sweets can further be seen (p.40) as symbolising all the
good things which seem to be safe from Krogstad's threats, when
Nora realises what she thinks will be the extent of Helmer's
influence in his new post. Later, when Nora is trying to prevent
Helmer from opening his letters (which involves persuading him to
do as she wishes) the macaroons are what Nora chooses to make
her point with when she orders the maid to 'Put out some
macaroons! Lots of macaroons — for once!' (p.78). Being prepared

to brave her husband's schoolmasterly anger, her action speaks of
the bravado of the child who knows her naughtiness must be
discovered.

Despite the realistic appearance of the set as described by Ibsen,
the playwright employs an essentially unrealistic use of lighting to
counterpoint and reinforce the reactions of his characters. When
Nora calls for the lamp (p.68), the ensuing light chases away more
than the physical gloom. She asks Dr. Rank: 'Aren't you ashamed
of yourself, now that the lamp's been lit?' (p.69). She is consciously
equating his declaration of love with the deeds of darkness even
though she has been prepared to exploit that gloom for her own
purposes.

A quite different technique is demonstrated, however, in Ibsen's
use of what the critic, John Northam, terms 'illustrative action'
(*Ibsen's Dramatic Method*, Faber). Rank comes to leave his final
visiting card:

> NORA (*strikes a match*). Let me give you a light.
> RANK. Thank you. (*She holds out the match for him. He
> lights his cigar.*) And now — goodbye. (p.90)

Thus the close sympathy between Nora and Dr. Rank can culminate
in a cryptic conversation, the words of which can quite credibly be
misunderstood by Helmer. The accompanying action, however,
contains the reality of the final farewell, a reality hidden behind
the illusion of everyday speech. At the same time Rank's tendency,
evident in the black crosses on his visiting cards as well as in the
example just cited, to regard himself and his actions symbolically
betrays an over-developed and crass sense of self-importance.

An early critic declared that 'the tarantella is the play', a
somewhat sweeping statement but one which draws attention to
the most obviously symbolic action in the play. In an effort to
prevent Helmer taking Krogstad's letter from the letter box, Nora
stages a rehearsal of the wild dance Helmer taught her. Although
the audience is privy to her emotional state, Helmer and Dr. Rank
must remain ignorant. Ibsen heightens the pathos and irony of
Nora's dilemma in his very choice of dance: a tarantella was
originally performed by those who were victims of the tarantula, a
supposedly poisonous spider. By such means is the emotional
power of the play kept on a par with that of poetic drama.

When Nora rehearses the tarantella she is wearing 'a long multi-
coloured shawl' (p.77); for the actual performance at the party she
has 'a large black shawl' (p.84). Such differences in appearance are

of crucial significance in the play. The colourful shawl would seem to embody a desire to cling to the many delights of life in the midst of the 'Dance of Life and Death' which is the Tarantella. By contrast the black shawl conceals the colourful Italian fancy-dress costume. Intuitively an audience responds to such visual symbolism; there is no need for the characters to express it in words. Nora's romantic reaction to Helmer's opening of the letter is contained as much in her wrapping of herself in his black cloak and her black shawl as she apparently rushes to commit suicide as it is in any of her statements. Conversely, when she re-appears to tell Helmer of her decision to leave him, she has removed the fancy dress and put on her everyday clothes. There are no illusions left. Nora must lay aside her world of child-like play to discover her own true identity. The costume, which has been painstakingly mended by Mrs. Linde at Nora's request as if in a last attempt to hide behind the mask of make-believe, is finally rejected.

Even such basic stage properties as doors are used by Ibsen to reinforce the themes of the play. There are nearly forty references to doors opening and closing in the stage directions and dialogue. The play begins with a door opening and ends with a door slamming shut. The door imagery throughout relates to themes of caged and free animals; to open and to closed possibilities; to the potentiality for change and its impossibility; to a sense of choices freely made and choices irrevocably determined by heredity and by social and environmental pressures.

Characters

Nora

When Nora first appears in the Helmers' comfortably and tastefully furnished living-room, she seems the perfect bourgeois wife. Returning laden with parcels from a shopping excursion, she is humming contentedly and tips the porter over-generously. Wrapped in furs to protect her from the cold, she resembles the 'squirrel' her husband calls her, returning to its drey laden with its hoard of supplies. Her girlish extravagance is established in her desire to spend Helmer's higher salary straight away, even though it will not actually materialise for a further three months. His disinclination to run up debts provokes her to sulk, the first example of Nora deliberately using her moodiness to get her own way. Helmer makes amends by giving her extra money for the Christmas expenses. Their relationship rests upon his paternalism and her

childlike qualities and is very much that of parent and child; when
he 'takes her playfully by the ear' (p.24), it is the action of an
adult dealing with a naughty infant. Her concealment of the fact
that she has been eating macaroons (when he has expressly
forbidden her to eat sweet things) is typical behaviour of a child,
but it is obvious that this episode is part of a ritual that the two of
them play, and which seems essential to their marriage.

Nora enjoys her role as spoilt child, relishing, too, her husband's
use of pet names. She delights in the power her attractiveness and
sexuality give her. When Helmer seems reluctant to fall in with her
wishes, she tries to wheedle the decision she wants out of him.
Despite such behaviour, Nora does intuitively apprehend the nature
of her marriage. She may seem superficially 'silly' but she knows
that to tell Helmer the truth would be to 'completely wreck our
relationship. This life we have built together would no longer exist'
(p.36). She prefers, however, deliberately to refrain from thinking
or talking about the reality of her situation. Thus, although she
hopes for and apparently expects a 'miracle', her responses are
rendered ambiguously complex because of the awareness which she
chooses to repress. It is vital to realise that the play is concerned to
show how Nora is compelled to face the implications of her
intuition which she has steadfastly tried to avoid acknowledging.

This refusal is further extended in Nora's conversation with Dr.
Rank in Act Two (p.64 onwards). Her seemingly callous reception
of the news of her friend's imminent death (because it makes it
more difficult for her to ask him to pay off the debt) is followed
by her equally clumsy flirtation with him and it becomes obvious
that Nora's interaction with others has always rested upon her
refusal even to think about, let alone understand how her actions
might affect other people. What upsets her is not that Rank loves
her but that he tells her, for this makes it impossible for her to
pretend ignorance of the impact of her conduct. She would rather
cling selfishly to behaviour she has delighted in from childhood as
her only means of escaping from the suffocating paternalism of,
first, her father and, now, her husband. Her liveliness demands an
outlet in lighthearted conversation and fun; unfortunately within
her circumscribed lifestyle, this can apparently be achieved only by
indulging in such immature behaviour.

The cosiness and peacefulness of the Helmers' home life
depends upon keeping any unpleasantness at a distance. Nora finds
it incomprehensible that society would prosecute her for an action
performed 'for love'. Her impulsiveness is at odds with that

society's narrow rules of conduct. Her superstitious, irrational nature is demonstrated when she desperately tries to ward off Krogstad's threats by busying herself with decorating the Christmas tree. She invokes all the ways in which she will entertain her husband, rather in the manner of a magic spell to ward off evil. Nora parades her practicality when she talks to Mrs. Linde in Act One, proud that she was able to find the money for Helmer's convalescence. She is, however, essentially *im*practical. There was no other thought in her mind than to 'save' her husband; therefore she did not think in advance about how the debt would be repaid or even about the possible results of committing the forgery. Similarly she cannot think coherently about how to deal with Krogstad's threats but lurches agonisingly from one hoped-for solution to the next without any properly formulated plan of action.

The interlude with the children shows Nora in the role of mother, but a mother whose love reveals itself in the form of play. She undresses the children because 'it's such fun' (p.43) and enters enthusiastically into the game of hide-and-seek. Her conversation with Anne-Marie, her old nanny, reveals her concern for the welfare of her children, but it should be remembered that a mother in a middle-class, nineteenth-century family was not concerned with the day-to-day care of the children. What they ate and wore, how they learnt, how they interacted with other people would be the nanny's concern. In such a situation, Nora's decision to leave home and entrust her children's lives to Anne-Marie would be far less disruptive and potentially damaging to her children than would now be the case. This is not to say that it was any the less shocking to contemporary audiences, as can be seen from the pressures placed upon Ibsen to write a 'happy ending', but Nora's final description of her children as having been 'dolls' is borne out by her earlier conduct.

Throughout the play Nora adopts a series of poses. With Helmer she is the child-wife who uses her sexuality to get her own way and is pleased to be protected and pampered. With Mrs. Linde she portrays herself as an energetic and supportive wife, capable of independent thought and action. With Rank, she is the flirtatious, amusing, youthful companion. Although her restlessness signals her basic insecurity and anxiety, she delights in her ability to manipulate. It is as if she were attempting to impose her own pattern upon a life that she knows subconsciously to be shaped by the forces at work in society which have pre-determined her roles of wife and mother. As Nora is propelled further and further into despair, she takes refuge in melodramatic posturing. Her agony is genuine (as shown by her fragmented soliloquies) but her actions betray a romantic desire to act 'heroically'. Thus her intention to commit suicide, cruelly but accurately dismissed by Helmer, is the climax of a life of self-deceit. When Nora re-appears clad in her everyday clothes, her apparently simple reply 'Yes, Torvald. I've changed' (p.96) is charged with both significance and pathos for now she must try to behave genuinely. The songbird has been forced to acknowledge what she has always known about life within this particular cage.

The first and final serious talk between Nora and Helmer represents a reversal in their previous roles. Now Nora takes the lead, forcing Helmer to look at their marriage from a totally new perspective. Explaining her new understanding that 'our home has never been anything but a playroom' (p.98) where 'In eight whole years . . . we have never exchanged a serious word on a serious subject' (p.97), she knows that she must now educate herself, that she can no longer live her life as somebody else's property. The only way to do this, she feels, is to leave Helmer and the children and 'stand on my own feet' (p.99). Her discussion of her position reveals an intuitive intelligence which has led her to connive at her own oppression since this had seemed the easiest way to a comfortable life. Faced with the most uncomfortable reality of the social, religious and moral codes which her husband represents, her energy and love of life, which so far have been channelled into frivolous enjoyment, come into their own. She can no longer love Helmer for he is not the man she had believed him to be. Despite his attempts to persuade her to stay, or at least remain in contact with him, Nora no longer believes in miracles. Handing back her wedding ring, the symbol of their marriage, she leaves, her claim for independence complete. As the sound of the slammed street door reverberates, Nora escapes to face the challenge of reality, a challenge which she is at least prepared to face, although she may be ill-equipped to win the fight.

Torvald Helmer

Torvald Helmer sees himself as the epitome of the respectable nineteenth-century husband. He treats his wife as a winsome little creature, capable of playful deception but dependent upon his largesse and knowledge of the outside world. Although he chastises her for being extravagant, he delights in being able to give her presents of money. One of the most obvious ways in which he maintains his dominance over Nora lies in his financial control of the household; ironically it is his refusal to compromise his honour by borrowing money that gives Nora the chance to prove her own ingenuity and love as well as ultimately destroying their security.

Helmer's apparent pomposity and lack of perception are the stereotyped response of the domestic male to his role. His patronising or teasing tone whenever he addresses Nora does not let up even in the face of her distress — that is, until she demands that they talk seriously. His security depends upon feeling superior. The games he and Nora play all seem designed to maintain his role as dominant male. She has learnt her own stereotyped role as subordinate sustainer of a man's self-opinion, and Helmer is the happy recipient of her expertise. As Nora says, 'he's so proud of being a man' (p.36), and yet it is this very pride which ensures that the miracle she expects can never happen.

In his treatment of Krogstad, Helmer reveals his essential pettiness so explicitly that even Nora cannot avoid it. Helmer's principal preoccupation is always with himself, so the idea that Krogstad might cause Helmer embarrassment by using his Christian name (p.62) is, in Helmer's view, more than enough reason to sack him. At the same time it needs to be noted that both Krogstad and Helmer have been found guilty of social indiscretions in the past so that it is not a simple case of social snobbery but rather the result of Helmer's desire not to be confronted by a mirror-image of himself. Similarly, although Helmer is driven by his desire for social approval and status and is more concerned with appearances than truth, there is also a sense that Helmer has perceived the absurdity which underlies social attitudes and mores (p.52). The one time in the past when he acted 'dishonourably' was in concealing the truth about Nora's father when he was appointed by the government to investigate a scandal. He is prepared, having scolded Nora, to revert to the status quo once the IOU is destroyed. If Nora had accepted, Helmer would have been happy since his social standing and respectability would not have been affected.

Quite apart from, and yet of a piece with, his behaviour towards his wife, Helmer is disagreeably patronising towards Mrs. Linde. He high-handedly acts the beneficent patron in agreeing to secure her employment (p.42) and later dismisses her pompously and unfairly as a 'dreadful bore' (p.87). Even more unpleasant is his selfishness in the face of Nora's news of the imminent death of Dr. Rank,

Helmer's friend. Rank's 'suffering and loneliness' are dismissed as merely 'a kind of dark background to the happy sunlight of our marriage' (p.91), which enables Helmer to switch back to his main preoccupation which at this point is to make love to his wife. When Nora objects, using Rank's death as a defence, Helmer pronounces pretentiously: 'You're right. This news has upset us both. An ugliness has come between us; thoughts of death and dissolution' (p.92). Even the knowledge that his friend is about to die cannot force him to alter his self-contained, self-obsessed perception of the world.

Ibsen's friend, the critic and dramatist, Bjoernstjerne Bjoernson, had written, in 1865, *The Newly Wedded Couple*, a play which concentrates upon the way in which the male, rather than the female, partner is treated as a mannequin. It is similarly a mistake to see *A Doll's House* solely as the tragedy of the female. Helmer holds rigid views, obsessed with the need to abide by the social, religious and moral code of the time but he is not presented unsympathetically. Nora has used his paternalism to her own advantage. Their marriage has depended upon her concealing, or refusing to acknowledge, that she does know the truth of her husband's character. Where Helmer is shown to be weak and in need of support, Nora's strong will and vitality enable her, finally, to cancel their marriage contract. Whereas he has suffered from overwork, financial insecurity and a certain amount of dishonour, she has been protected by her lack of involvement with the world. When Nora leaves Helmer, she abandons him to face the ensuing scandal. There is never any doubt that he believes that he loves Nora; his tragedy lies in failing to offer her anything other than a sentimental, protective form of love. He is as much a victim of his society's attitudes as Nora.

Nils Krogstad

Krogstad is, in a superficial sense, the villain of the piece. Interrupting Nora's innocent game of hide-and-seek, he appears like the spectre at the feast — the malign influence who will destroy the family's peace and happiness. At first he asks Nora to use her influence with her husband (p.46) but, when she disclaims any such power, he is provoked into threatening to reveal all to Helmer. Knowing the ways of the world, a world against which he feels all the bitterness of a man who has been rejected, he carefully and delightedly reveals Nora's true situation to her. The drawn out process of question and answer (p.47-8) by which he demonstrates his detailed knowledge of her forgery underlines his unpleasant enjoyment of the fact that she is in his power. By experience he has learnt the attitude of society towards such a crime: 'But I can assure you that it is no bigger nor worse a crime than the one I once committed and thereby ruined my whole social position' (p.49): A lawyer, he knows that 'the law does not concern itself with motives' and that Nora will have to reach some agreement with him.

After being rejected by Mrs. Linde, Krogstad had made an unhappy marriage. Now a widower with three children to bring up, he is determined to hold on to the respectability he has worked so hard to re-establish. Like Helmer he desires social position and prestige above all things. Krogstad understands Helmer's essential weakness and lack of courage. He is determined to exploit his position as Nora's creditor to his own financial and social benefit. He increases the stakes on his second visit to Nora (pp.70-3), when he demands that Helmer make him assistant manager. Convinced that Nora, like himself, would not have the courage to commit suicide, Krogstad tries to frighten her further by hinting forcefully at the effects of drowning (p.73), a description which lingers in Nora's imagination.

Despite Krogstad's catalogue of complaints against society, he remains the apparent embodiment of villainy until his dialogue with Mrs. Linde (pp.80-4). His bitterness at being jilted is gradually eroded as she explains her position and begs him to join his life with hers. His sense of the loss he felt when she rejected him is both poignant and forceful: 'When I lost you, it was just as though all solid ground had been swept from under my feet. Look at me. Now I'm a shipwrecked man, clinging to a spar' (p.81). The emotional despair humanises the stage villain, giving a different dimension to his actions and cynicism. At first he dismisses Mrs. Linde's plea as 'hysterical and romantic' (p.82), accusing her of wanting to find an excuse for self-sacrifice. Once he is convinced that she is genuine, his joy is instantaneous. As a result he no longer wishes to hurt Nora but accepts unquestioningly Mrs. Linde's suggestion that it would be better for Helmer to know the truth. The 'villain' departs the happiest man in the world, leaving his letter untouched.

Doctor Rank

Rank is a close family friend; it is understood that he will join the family's Christmas celebrations (p.27). His tone of cynical bitterness finds expression in the first conversation with Nora when, having described the successful Krogstad as a moral cripple, he extends his remarks to include society in general — those who are corrupt are given 'some nice, comfortable position' while 'the healthy ones just have to lump it' (p.40). Thus, in Rank's view, human society is being turned into 'a hospital'.

In love with Nora, he chooses to confide in her that he will soon die. He is suffering from tuberculosis of the spine, inherited from his father who had venereal disease as a result of a debauched life. Rank knows he is about to enter upon the phase of 'final disintegration' (p.65). Realising Helmer is 'sensitive' and 'hates anything ugly', he does not want his friend to visit him in hospital. He will send a visiting card with a black cross on it to tell Nora when 'the final filthy process has begun'. His disgust and bitterness at his lot are intense and he is jealous that Mrs. Linde will very rapidly take his place as the family friend. When Nora flirts outrageously with him as a prelude to asking him for money, he chooses this moment to declare his love for her, a love that has been concealed behind banter and amusement. He is surprised by Nora's reaction, which suggests that she knew how he felt but did not want it openly declared (p.68). He finds her impossible to understand but continues to show affection and support, even though she carelessly wounds him by equating his company with that of the servants when she was a child.

There is also something comic about Rank. The detached scientific curiosity with which he regards his own demise — even to the extent of conducting experiments on himself — suggests a macabre fascination with the processes of illness and death. His rather portentous use of the symbolic phrase 'and thank you for the light' (p.90), his penchant for black, and the crosses on the visiting cards perhaps almost justify the indifference with which the news of his imminent death is received. He has been like a member of the living dead extracting whatever life he can from his fleeting encounters with Nora.

Mrs. Christine Linde

Widowed and released from the burden of an ailing mother and two younger brothers, Mrs. Linde, an old school friend of Nora's, finds herself free at last. Ironically that very freedom which she had so much desired when married to a man she did not love proves irksome. Her life has been more difficult than it might have been because of her sense of duty, that duty which determined that she should break with Krogstad, whom she loved, because he had no money with which to maintain her family. Through having to work, she has discovered that she 'must work if I'm to find life worth living' (p.82), but work on its own is not enough. Her freedom she now perceives as loneliness, for she feels 'so dreadfully lost and empty'. She desperately wants 'something — someone — to work for', as she pleads to Krogstad. She, unlike Nora, has had to face the world and survive on her own. She knows the value of the support of another human being: 'Castaways have a better chance of survival together than on their own.'

Throughout her conversations with Nora, Mrs. Linde seems older and wiser than her frivolous, extravagant schoolfriend. She acts the role of motherly confidante, alternately patronising and chiding Nora. Although she is prepared to intervene with Krogstad on Nora's behalf, it is Christine Linde who prevents him from asking Helmer for the return of the letter. Her conversations with Nora have led her to the conclusion that 'There must be an end of all these shiftings and evasions' (p.84). If Nora and Helmer are to achieve a 'full understanding', Helmer must know the truth of Nora's secret dealings. Thus it is Christine's influence on Krogstad which both creates the possibility of a 'happy ending' and ensures that Nora will be forced to confront the truth of her husband's nature and her own situation. When Nora slams the door, she is deliberately choosing the kind of life represented by Mrs. Linde and from which Mrs. Linde is trying to escape. Her hard life has fostered an idealism based on a concept of 'truth' which blinds her to the fact that the security of illusions may be preferable to the choice which Nora eventually feels she has to make. There is irony in the fact that Mrs. Linde's idealistic motivation leads to the break-up of Nora's marriage, when it was designed to establish it on a firmer basis.

Anne-Marie, the Nurse

Having brought up Nora, Anne-Marie is now nanny to Nora's children. Her history is common to the nineteenth century. She gave up her own illegitimate child to strangers in order to take up the offer of a job as 'wet-nurse' and nanny to Nora. She is down-to-earth and 'reasonable', accepting her position in society and critical only of the father of her child — 'That good-for-nothing didn't lift a finger' (p.56). She is protective towards Nora and indispensable. The nineteenth-century middle-class family depended upon such servants. Nora plays with her children and

buys them presents; Anne-Marie looks after them and brings them
up.

The children

For practical reasons the children are often cut from performance.
Ibsen has facilitated this by giving all their dialogue to Nora. If this
is the case, however, it is crucial that the lines Nora speaks to them
and her playing of hide-and-seek should still be included by having
the children apparently present off-stage. The children are Nora's
'dolls'. She delights in playing with them. They have no designated
characters but perform an important function in the play by
actually showing Nora in the role of mother.

Under protest, Ibsen provided an alternative ending to the play
in which Nora melodramatically revokes her decision to leave,
under emotional pressure from Helmer who exploits the fact of the
children:

NORA. . . . that our life together could become a real marriage.
Good-bye. (*She starts to go.*)
HELMER. Go then! (*he seizes her arm.*) But first you shall see
your children for the last time.
NORA. Let me go! I will not see them. I cannot!
HELMER (*dragging her to the door on the left*). You shall see
them! (*He opens the door and says softly:*) Look – there
they are, sleeping peacefully and without care. Tomorrow,
when they wake and call for their mother, they will be . . .
motherless!
NORA (*trembling*). Motherless!
HELMER. As you once were.
NORA. Motherless! (*After an inner struggle, she lets her bag
fall, and says:*) Ah, though it is a sin against myself, I cannot
leave them! (*She sinks almost to the ground by the door.*)

The curtain falls.

(Trans. Peter Watts, Penguin, p.334)

Ibsen called this a 'barbaric outrage' on the play but it serves to
demonstrate the importance of the idea of the children even if
their presence is minimal. In fact, the 'non-existence' of the
children is an aspect of their reality. In earlier drafts they were
assigned individual lines but Ibsen gradually eliminated them
individually until they became 'the children'. Their reality is
conferred on them by Nora, who ventriloquises their responses. It

is not simply a convenient device for getting round the staging problem. The 'sexist' lines of their conventional upbringing should also be noted — a doll for Emmy, a sword for Ivar. It is tempting to see Emmy's destructiveness — 'she'll pull them apart in a few days' (p.25) — as a form of rebellion.

Themes

A Feminist Tract?

An important contemporary of Ibsen, the Swedish dramatist, August Strindberg, thought *A Doll's House* an outrageous defence of feminism and an act of male treachery on Ibsen's part (see his Preface to *Getting Married*). The play has been repeatedly both acclaimed and vilified as advocating women's liberation, a matter which had been under public discussion in Norway, as elsewhere, during the nineteenth century. In 1869 Georg Brandes, the Danish critic had translated J.S. Mill's *The Subjection of Women* and in 1871 Mathilde Schjoett wrote *The Women-Friends' Discussion of 'The Subjection of Women'*. The sensational impact of *A Doll's House* when it was first produced at the Theatre Royal, Copenhagen demonstrates just how radical the drama was in its sympathetic portrayal of a woman who refuses to obey her husband, leaving him, her home and her children. Ibsen himself, however, insisted that he was 'more of a poet and less of a social philosopher' (speech to the Norwegian Association for Women's Rights in Christiania, 26 May 1898) and that he was not 'even very sure what Women's Rights really are'. His interest lay not in specific political and social changes but in a 'revolution of the spirit of man'. While writing *A Doll's House* Ibsen made the following notes:

There are two kinds of moral laws, two kinds of conscience, one for men and one, quite different, for women. They don't understand each other; but in practical life, woman is judged by masculine law, as though she weren't a woman but a man.

The wife in the play ends by having no idea what is right and what is wrong; natural feelings on the one hand and belief in authority on the other lead her to utter distraction.

A woman cannot be herself in modern society. It is an exclusively male society, with laws made by men and with prosecutors and judges who assess female conduct from a male standpoint.

She has committed forgery, which is her pride; for she has

done it out of love for her husband, to save his life. But this husband of hers takes his standpoint, conventionally honourable, on the side of the law, and sees the situation with male eyes.

Moral conflict. Weighed down and confused by her trust in authority, she loses faith in her own morality, and in her fitness to bring up her children. Bitterness. A mother in modern society, like certain insects, retires and dies once she has done her duty by propagating the race. Love of life, of home, of husband and children and family. Now and then, as women do, she shrugs off her thoughts. Suddenly anguish and fear return. Everything must be borne alone. The catastrophe approaches, mercilessly, inevitably. Despair, conflict and defeat.

Nora represents the middle-class, nineteenth-century daughter and wife who is 'protected' from experiencing the hardships (and benefits) of the world outside the family and is expected to suppress her own desires in deference to the wishes of first, her father, and then her husband. Women's liberation is, however, not the main concern of A Doll's House; the plight of women is part of a larger theme, the necessity for *self*-liberation. Both Nora and Helmer are victims of their social roles as husband and wife. In attempting to behave according to convention, they have developed a marriage which is based upon an illusion. Within their relationship they deceive each other and themselves both consciously and sub-consciously. Nora does not see the forgery as anything but a means to an end and engages in it almost casually without realising its full social consequences. Her priority is the welfare of her husband. The irony is that the forgery, the most glaring of a whole sequence of 'shiftings and evasions' (p.84), can be seen as the one genuine act of love in the whole play.

Desperately wanting to be the conventional good wife, Nora has wilfully learned to suppress those areas of her consciousness which lead her, ultimately, to reject Helmer and what he stands for. Dreaming of improbable solutions to her problem — Dr. Rank will leave her money, Helmer will take the weight of the world's accusations upon his own shoulders — she tries to maintain the fragile foundations of her life with Helmer. Suddenly, when he does not behave in the hoped-for miraculous fashion, she is confronted by what she has always suspected — her husband's subservience to petty social values which are more important to him than his feelings for his wife.

Helmer, however, is trapped in *his* social role. Afraid of any repetition of social humiliation just prior to his new appointment, he can only mouth his desires to be brave, honest and responsible. He repeatedly asserts that his honour is of paramount importance but this is equated merely with social respectability. Once the danger from Krogstad has receded, he wishes to reassume his role as protector — 'I shall watch over you like a hunted dove which I have snatched unharmed from the claws of the falcon' (p.96). This indeed sounds like the heroic defender whom Nora at first thought — and then hoped — she had married. But he has revealed his inadequacy in so stark a fashion that not even Nora can hide from the reality of her husband's motives and attitudes. In these circumstances, Nora comes to realise (perhaps too suddenly for much faith to be invested in the maturity of her decision) the hollow sham that has been their life together. The passion, ingenuity and courage which she has so far channelled into her attempts at acting the role of dutiful wife and mother now seek an alternative outlet. No longer prepared to accept marriage to a man who 'just thought it was fun to be in love' (p.98) and who expects her simply to mirror his tastes and attitudes, she claims the right to educate herself — 'I must think things out for myself, and try to find my own answer' (p.100) — and the right to discover 'which is right, society or I' (p.101). Shocked by the experience of what she has found out about certain laws which would condemn her as a criminal when she only sought to save her husband's life, Nora begins to question the demands of duty to her husband and children as expounded by religion and society when they run counter to her duty towards herself.

Love and duty: self-liberation

In the character of Mrs. Linde, Ibsen presents the results of a marriage embarked upon purely out of duty to members of one's family. For the sake of her sick, ageing mother and two younger brothers, she married a man whom she did not love but whose wealth would bring her family financial security. This might appear praiseworthy but it has ultimately brought her only misery. Seeing herself as a 'shipwrecked soul' with the opportunity of choosing whom to share her life with, Mrs. Linde makes a determined bid to re-establish herself in Krogstad's affections. At first glance this reuniting of the two lovers can seem to present a rather romantic view of love as conqueror. However, Christine has 'learned to look at things practically' (p.81). She does not rush back to Krogstad

because he is her one true love. Her experience of life and poverty
has forced her to earn her own living and become financially
independent but has left her feeling 'so dreadfully lost and empty'
(p.82). Ironically where Nora flies to the world outside to discover
her own identity, Christine 'couldn't bear to stay out there any
longer' and chooses the safety of domesticity. It may not be a
particularly laudable decision — in some ways she seems about to
repeat a version of her former mistake in marrying for security and
in order to look after another — but it shows her to be aware of all
the issues involved in making such a decision which is based on her
individual needs. Nora, too, must be allowed time and room to
grow into an independent being whose decisions will be her own.

In *A Doll's House* Ibsen shows romantic love to be a delusion,
inhibiting the free development of the individual. To keep Helmer's
love, Nora lies, pretends to be helpless and suppresses her true
feelings, expecting the time to arrive when Helmer will no longer
love her because she has lost her physical beauty (p.36). Helmer is
as blinded by ideas of love as Nora. Treating her like an errant
child, commenting on her wastefulness and helplessness, he claims
to love her. His sexual appetite is quickened by her beauty,
particularly when it is being appreciated by others (p.88). He
thinks of Nora as 'my most treasured possession'. In striving to
maintain a romantic view of marriage, the two of them have
assumed roles in which they have gradually become trapped. When
Nora slams the door, she shatters the romantic masquerade that has
been their life.

Heredity and environment: determinism and free will
As part of the continuing debate about whether our lives are
shaped by our own free choice or determined by a combination of
our past and our environment, the nineteenth century witnessed
an increasing concern with individual liberty and social equality.
A Doll's House seems to illustrate the moral and psychological
need to exercise free will in situations where authority inhibits
personal development. The play's conclusion implies that
individuals need to be responsible for themselves and exercise
free will. However, there is a concomitant interest in the idea that
lives are determined by heredity and environment. *The Origin
of Species* (1859) by Charles Darwin (1809-82) propounded
the theory that animals, and therefore man, evolved according to
laws of natural selection which placed man in a hereditary
sequence which linked him with his ape-like ancestors. Within the

play Ibsen uses 'modern' ideas to dramatic effect. Dr. Rank, suffering from a disease inherited as a result of his father's overly indulgent life, takes a detached, scientific interest in the progress of his own ailments (pp.64-5). This sense that general truths about the human condition can only be arrived at by studying man's behaviour with the same kind of scientific detachment with which one studies the behaviour of animals reflects the influence of naturalist thought.

Helmer alludes to Nora having inherited her spendthrift ways from her father (p.26) and accuses her: 'all your father's recklessness and instability he has handed on to you!' (p.93). It is Helmer who is shown to be the one most deeply affected by his environment. Where Nora's domestic role, coupled with her natural vivacity and intelligence, enable her to reject the controlling influence of society, Helmer remains cowed by a social code he can neither live up to nor ignore. Nora's final action may prove to be the one catalyst which would force her husband to reassess his ability to decide actively for himself rather than rely passively upon social conventions. In such ways Ibsen champions the idea of individual spirit, integrity and potential. Because middle-class domesticity exists by ignoring basic problems of human existence, it can only prove to be a lie. Ibsen exposes the sham. His choice of the nature of Rank's illness emphasises the inner corruption of such a society.

Nora wants freedom in order to become an individual, freedom to do what she feels she must do; she has no sense of social obligations, community or political reforms. In a letter Ibsen wrote:

> Now there is absolutely no reasonable necessity for the individual to be a citizen. On the contrary, the state is the curse of the individual. The state must be abolished! In that revolution I will take part. Undermine the idea of the state; make willingness and spiritual kinship the only essentials in the case of a union — and you have the beginning of a liberty that is of some value . . .

Images

A Doll's House

A doll's house provides a make-believe world where children make their dolls perform social roles. Through the agency of the title and by means of various speeches within the play, Ibsen draws a

parallel between the life that is represented in the house on stage
and the false life of a doll's house. This is most clearly emphasised
when Nora describes herself as her husband's doll and the children
as *her* dolls. Helmer's paternalism seems to confirm this throughout
the play as he gives Nora presents expecting her to entertain him in
return. Under the guise of being a good mother, she plays games
with her children and gives them presents. Their real needs are
catered for by Anne-Marie. When Nora slams the door at the end of
the play, she is rejecting her role as a doll in order to realise her full
potential as an individual in the outside world.

The world of nature

Apart from the lines relating to 'dolls' and 'play', the most obvious
thread of imagery which runs through *A Doll's House* is that which
relates to the world of nature. The window in the left hand wall of
the set looks on to the outside world and the Scandinavian winter.
The cosy drawingroom, warmed by the large stove placed on the
opposite side of the stage, is a refuge from the weather which is
equated with the bleakness of human interaction in the world of
business. When Krogstad enters, he brings the cold with him. Mrs.
Linde's experiences of life outside have left her feeling empty and
lonely. By contrast, Nora has so far managed to protect her
sheltered haven from disruption. The deceit she has practised to
safeguard her home, eventually forces her out into the cold.
Helmer knows just how fragile is their protected environment —
one cruel stroke of fate could destroy it. The image chosen is of a
tile falling from a house on to his head — the result of a natural
storm could so easily bring financial ruin. By such means, Ibsen
establishes a finely balanced tension between the two worlds of
nature and social convention.

Both Krogstad and Mrs. Linde are described as 'castaways',
symbolic victims of a world of storm and tempest, as well as of the
cruel reality of a system based on finance and moral cowardice.
Their emotional condition is reflected in Mrs. Linde's description
of them as 'two shipwrecked souls' (p.82). Helmer's pet names for
Nora would also seem to ally her with the world of nature. The
creatures she is likened to, however, are essentially small, gentle
and pleasure-giving. The 'lark' and 'squirrel' have difficulty
surviving in a world where Nature seems, in Tennyson's words, 'red
in tooth and claw'. The imagery hence reinforces the audience's
ambivalent emotions when Nora finally slams the door. The
'expensive pet' (p.26) has now to cope with the natural world to

which it belongs and yet from which it has been alienated. There is no easy optimism available to the observer. The 'hunted dove' has refused to be 'snatched from the claws of the falcon' (p.96). Its survival must be problematic.

Looked at from the standpoint of the imagery of the play, it is less easy to dismiss Krogstad's warning to Nora about taking her own life as mere melodramatic rhetoric. The force of the terrifying effects of drowning gains in power from being part of a general imagery of storm and shipwreck. Ultimately, the natural world will exact retribution from those who cannot master its laws.

The 'miracle'

Another facet of Ibsen's ability to imbue language with poetic power can be seen in his development of Nora's use of the word 'miracle'. At first she regards their approaching prosperity as 'almost like a miracle', for it will release her from her debt, but once it becomes clear that the facts of the whole episode will be made public, she describes herself as 'sitting here and waiting for the miracle to happen' (p.79). The 'miracle' has changed its substance and now consists of Helmer taking entire responsibility for her action upon himself. When 'the miracle failed to happen' (p.101), Nora is forced to acknowledge what she has concealed in her subconscious — the true nature of her husband and her relationship with him. Her husband has embodied her religion. Helmer has been the God-like provider upon whom she has depended totally, accepting his wishes and attitudes as innately superior to her own. She uses the word 'miracle' several times in her final conversation with Helmer. Once her belief in him is broken, she has no concept of religious duty left. The 'miracle of miracles' (p.104) would now mean both she and Helmer undergoing such revolutionary changes in character that their union could become a genuine marriage. Thus, Ibsen's development of Nora's concept of 'the miracle' in itself charts her progress towards self-realisation. Helmer's plight is poignantly reinforced when his last hope of 'The miracle of miracles —?' (p.104) is shattered by the slamming of the front door.

Ibsen's influence

Although many of Ibsen's plays when first performed or published created a furore amongst critics and certain sections of the public, they also enjoyed enormous popularity and support amongst progressive young writers and theatre directors all over Europe. In

England the leading critical supporters of Ibsen were Edmund
Gosse, William Archer, J.T. Grein and George Bernard Shaw,
who battled to undermine the arguments of conservative critics
such as Clement Scott, writing for the *Daily Telegraph,* who had
accused Ibsen of producing degrading, sensationalist filth. 'By the
late 1890s Ibsen's detractors all over Europe were largely silent
and his supporters triumphantly welcomed his growing stature as a
dramatist of international repute' (David Thomas, *Henrik Ibsen,*
Macmillan, pp.158-9).

Ibsen's work has directly and indirectly influenced a vast array
of successive playwrights. It was Ibsen's example that inspired
G.B. Shaw to write his early didactic plays such as *Widowers'*
Houses (1892) and *Mrs. Warren's Profession* (1893), which deal
with social problems and moral issues. The line of influence in the
British theatre, embracing such figures as Pinero, Galsworthy and
Rattigan on the way, remains strong today. The Irish dramatists,
J.M. Synge (1871-1909) and Sean O'Casey (1880-1964)
consciously used their debt to Ibsen, the former in his depiction of
Nora, the young wife, in *In the Shadow of the Glen* and the latter
in *The Plough and the Stars* where the scenes between Jack
Clitheroe and Nora recall those between Nora and Helmer. Synge
attacked Ibsen for removing the crucial element of 'joy' from the
stage but nevertheless acknowledged the advances introduced by
the Norwegian in terms of subject matter and technique. This is
especially clear in *The Playboy of the Western World,* which owes
a strong debt to *Peer Gynt.*

Ibsen's impact on later writers has varied enormously. Open
admiration is the case of Arthur Miller whose *All My Sons* (1947)
provides a variation on the theme of *Pillars of Society* and whose
Death of a Salesman (1949) is probably the most celebrated
attempt, through the character of Willy Loman, to extend Ibsen's
concept of tragedy. Both plays also make much use of Ibsen's
retrospective technique. Even Bertolt Brecht (1898-1956), who
thought that 'a modern spectator can't learn anything from them'
(*Brecht on Theatre,* Methuen, p.66), considered Ibsen's plays
'important historical documents'. And Chekhov, as David Thomas
points out, 'quite brilliantly adapted Ibsen's technique to serve his
own very different needs and aspirations as a writer' (Thomas,
p.160). The influence of *The Wild Duck* on the writing of *The*
Seagull is clear.

For Ibsen's younger contemporaries in Germany *A Doll's House*
provided a much needed focus for their desire to change the arid

mechanistic approach embodied in the established theatres. Frowned upon, and frequently censored by, the German authorities, Ibsen's work encouraged such as Gerhart Hauptmann to address themselves to serious social themes avoiding conventional stereotypes and obligatory happy endings. European drama could no longer pretend to be separate from real life; the long reign of melodrama and romanticism had been challenged by Ibsen's intentions and achievements. His plays are a seminal influence in the development of modern theatre. *A Doll's House* acted as 'a clarion call to the younger generation of dramatic realists' (Allardyce Nicoll, *World Drama*, Harrap, p.536). It was a clarion call that effectively changed the face of European theatre practice and playwriting.

Nora in Act Three

Productions of *A Doll's House*

Continental productions

The world premiere of *A Doll's House* was given in Denmark, at the
Royal Theatre, Copenhagen, on 21 December 1879, directed by H.P.
Holst after only two blocking and eight general rehearsals. Betty
Hennings played Nora and the production, despite its conventional
setting and inadequate preparation, ran for twenty-one performances
during that season alone. It remained in the repertory for all of
twenty-eight years, to be revived in all its essentials as late as 1955.
Critical attention focused on the morality of the play's ending and
especially Nora's decision to abandon her three children. Doubts
were also expressed about the plausibility of Nora's psychological
'revolution' during the play's final scene when she undergoes an
apparently instantaneous transformation from doll-wife to mature
woman. According to one newspaper critic, 'Nora has only shown
herself as a little Fordic "Frou-Frou" and as such she cannot be
transformed in a flash to a Soren Kierkegaard in skirts' (cited in F.J.
and L-L. Marker, *Ibsen's Lively Art*, CUP, 1989, p. 48). Despite his,
critics were generally very impressed by the production and
especially the childlike quality of the twenty-nine-year-old
Hennings' performance. Reflecting later on this production, and
comparing her performance with others he had seen over the years,
the English journalist and writer, Maurice Baring, commented that
'She made the transformation [...] of the Nora of the first act into
the Nora of the last act seem the most natural thing in the world'
(ibid., p. 50).

The first production in Ibsen's native Norway was given the
following year at the Christiania Theatre, in what is now Oslo, with
Johanne Juell as a Nora who brought a touch of wild hysteria to the
role in what was otherwise a rather slapdash production by all
accounts, which ran for only twenty-eight performances.

In Germany, the first production of *A Doll's House* was staged at
the Residenz Theater, Munich, in 1880, directed by Ernst von
Possart, with Marie Ramlo as Nora. Ibsen saw the production and
said that he felt 'a couple of actors had not fully understood their
roles [and that] he did not like the wallpaper in the living room'
(Ferguson, 1996, pp. 246–7). Although this production had
conformed to Ibsen's original, his German translator had warned
him in advance of German audiences' potential response to the
play's liberationist ending. Much against his will, Ibsen felt obliged
to compose an alternative ending to suit bourgeois taste, which he

described as 'an act of barbarous violence against the play', but which he preferred to write himself rather than allow anyone else to do it. In this revised version, Helmer drags Nora to the bedroom door and, pointing to their sleeping children, demands she consider what they would feel like when they realise they are 'motherless'. Whereupon, overcome with remorse, she recants as follows:

> Motherless! (*After an inner struggle, she lets her bag fall, and says*) Ah, though it is a sin against myself, I cannot leave them! *She sinks almost to the ground by the door. The curtain falls.*

According to Robert Ferguson,

> Since the author himself had written it, many German theatres used the new ending. Hedwig Niemann-Raabe performed the barbarism in Flensburg, Hamburg, Dresden and Hanover. She also performed it in Berlin, where there was such an outcry over the dishonesty that shortly afterwards the play had to be performed in its original version. This in turn provoked a second outcry, and a third version was performed, incorporating a putative 'missing' fourth act in which Fru Linde and Krogstad are discovered a married couple, with a restless Nora their guest. Torvald arrives. Nora looks up at him and whispers 'Have you then quite forgiven me?' Helmer gives her a mysterious but affectionate look, takes out a large bag of the forbidden macaroons and pops one into her mouth with a smile. 'The miracle of miracles!' cries Nora joyfully, as the curtain descends. (Ibid., p. 245)

Irene Triesch played Nora in a production at the Lessing Theatre, Berlin, in 1889, staged by Otto Brahm, a director famed for his naturalistic approach. According to one critic, the actress gave the impression of 'a sleepwalker dancing on the edge of an abyss' (Marker and Marker, op. cit., p. 57), an interpretation which coloured Brahm's next production, at the Deutsches Theater, Berlin, in 1894, with Agnes Sorma as Nora. To many this seemed a savage, almost Strindbergian interpretation of the role in which the clash with Helmer brought out the sexual undercurrent in the relationship. The final scene was acted in such a way as to emphasise the complete humiliation of the husband in face of Nora's scornful contempt for his about-turn when he thinks he has been 'saved' from public exposure. In this connection it is interesting to note that Strindberg's third wife, Harriet Bosse, acted Nora when aged fifty, at the Royal

Dramatic Theatre, Stockholm, in 1925.

One of the first great European actresses to tackle the role was the Italian Eleonore Duse, at the Teatro di Filodrammatici, Milan, in 1891, using a heavily cut text which, among other things, omitted the children. While some critics criticised the cuts and Duse's tendency to over-domesticate the role, others appreciated the subtlety with which she handled the more melodramatic moments, such as the tarantella, performed wearing a crown of roses and executed with just a few, tentative steps before collapsing in an apparent paroxysm of nervous exhaustion. The noted Ibsen translator, William Archer, who saw the production on tour at the Lyric Theatre, London, in 1893, was struck by an almost expressionisitc effect at the beginning of the last act when Duse appeared hollow-eyed and ashen-faced as if 'the shadow of death' lay over her. After seeing her performance in Vienna, the poet and librettist Hugo von Hofmannsthal 'compared the contrast between her martyred feelings and her calm self-possession to that of a passion-play actor in the role of Jesus Christ' (Simon Williams, 'Ibsen and the theatre 1877–1900', in McFarland, 1994, p. 177).

The first French production was given in 1894 at the Théâtre de Vaudeville, in Paris, with Gabrielle Réjane as Nora. An actress of enormous nervous energy who had had a recent success in a boulevard play by Sardou, Réjane seemed an unlikely candidate for the role of Nora but managed to bring it off by emphasising the character's underlying sense of fear, combined with an innate eroticism which, finally, produced a sense of authentic revolt. Meanwhile, in Russia, the first production of *Nora* (as the play has tended to be called in that country) was staged by the entrepreneur F.A. Korsh at his own theatre in Moscow in 1882. The first St Petersburg production was in 1883, followed closely by one at the Aleksandrinsky Theatre, also in St Petersburg, the following year with Mariya Savina as Nora. However, the most famous Russian interpreter of the role was undoubtedly Vera Komissarzhevskaia who, having starred at the Aleksandrinsky in the ill-fated premiere of Chekhov's *The Seagull* in 1896, subsequently established her own theatre, in St Petersburg, where she staged *A Doll's House* in 1904, at the age of forty. While her own performance was a triumph and she was literally bombarded with flowers at the final curtain, Nikolai Krasov's Helmer seemed to critics a very weak foil to this powerful actress who, when she later toured America, was praised for 'that rare power of showing the working of one emotion beneath another' in a manner that was 'simply wonderful! Wonderful!' and where 'superb acting brought out Nora in a new psychological light' (cited in Victor Borovsky, *A Triptych from the Russian Theatre*, London, Hurst & Co., 2001, p. 199).

A further production of the play at Korsh's Theatre, Moscow, in 1891, was followed by one at the theatre owned and run by Chekhov's friend, the publisher and entrepreneur Aleksei Suvorin, in St Petersburg, with Lydia Yavorska as Nora. Komissarzhevskaia then revived the play at her own theatre to which she had invited the comparatively unknown director (at that stage in his illustrious career) Vsevolod Meyerhold. A former actor at the Moscow Art Theatre, Meyerhold had left to found his own company in 1902, subsequently spending three years working in the provinces where he achieved interesting results through applying theatrical techniques derived from his interest in Symbolist theories of theatre production. His production of *A Doll's House* in 1906 retained essentially the same decor as for the 1904 version but sought to stage the action more as a bas-relief, a technique he was to employ in more radical experimental productions involving Komissarzhevskaia, by confining all the action to the forward edge of the stage. The decor was stylised so that, instead of cosy bourgeois domesticity, the audience was confronted with what looked like a 'cramped corridor passageway with a decrepit piano in one corner [. . .], an equally dilapidated three-legged table [. . .], an arbitrarily suspended window [. . .] and cranberry-coloured drapes' (Marker and Marker, op. cit., pp. 63–4). Perhaps taking a leaf out of Duse's interpretative book, the tarantella was staged by Meyerhold as 'no more than a series of expressive poses during which the feet simply tapped out a nervous rhythm. If you watched only the feet, it looked more like running than dancing' (Edward Braun, ed., *Meyerhold on Theatre*, rev. edn., London, Methuen, 1991, p. 25).

Meyerhold went on to stage further productions of the play after the Russian Revolution, first in Petrograd (formerly St Petersburg) in 1918 and then in Novorossisk in 1920. However, probably the most radical version of the play ever mounted was the one he staged after three days' rehearsal in Moscow in 1922, at the former Nezlobin (renamed the Actor's Theatre) where his assistant – the future film director, Sergei Eisenstein – later recorded in his memoirs a sense of creative excitement such as he had experienced in his life neither before nor since. Audiences arrived at the venue to encounter a setting composed of stage flats which might normally have been used for a conventional naturalistic setting, but here reversed to reveal blank canvas with exposed wooden supports. They had been propped

against the stage walls in a state of complete disarray as if to suggest
that the domestic revolution which the play records had found its
counterpart in the political revolution taking place beyond the
theatre's walls.

Two of the finest Scandinavian interpreters of Nora have been, in
the 1930s, Tore Segelcke and, more recently, Liv Ullmann at the Det
Norske Teatret in 1974. The former's was 'a thoroughly, fiercely
modern portrayal of a distraught, self-possessed human being whose
"eerie gaiety" in the first act gave unmistakeable warning of the
angry rebelliousness and bitter disappointment that were to follow.
Her tarantella became "the outburst of a temperament rendered
unbalanced and rebellious by her sense of aloneness in a sexual
charade she had, deep down, always regarded as degrading"' (Marker
and Marker, op. cit., p. 70). Liv Ullmann's interpretation had the
great advantage of her having previously worked with the great
Swedish film director, Ingmar Bergman, for whom she had appeared
in several, emotionally rather bleak, films. While inheriting the
interpretation from Segelcke in many respects, Ullmann deliberately
suppressed the element of hope at the conclusion. The implication
here was that life in the outside world was more likely to lead to
the madhouse than to the achievement of any kind of genuine
independence.

Bergman himself had first turned his attention to the play in 1964
and then, more significantly, in 1981, with a production at the
Residenztheater, Munich, with Rita Russek as Nora. Rather like the
production of *Hedda Gabler* he had staged in London with Maggie
Smith in 1970, Bergman lined the non-representational box set in
dark red so that it seemed a womb-like limbo into which neither
light nor air penetrated. A succession of fragmentary settings were
indicated by a bare minimum of furniture and properties and the
final confrontation took place with Torvald lying on a brass bedstead
which was a full-sized replica of one of the toys which had earlier
been scattered across the front of the small stage platform. Another
device which Bergman employed was to have all the offstage figures
permanently and dimly discernible in a half-light surrounding the
main stage area into which they stepped when making an entrance,
rather like figures of fate, or role-players in a masquerade. In this
sense the production seemed reminiscent of Strindberg's *A Dream
Play*, which Bergman had previously directed, but with Nora as the
dreamer whose controlling consciousness dictated the nature of the
action. Her tarantella, danced on a tabletop, seemed like a cry for
help while, at the play's conclusion, as if waking from a bad dream,

Nora made her exit through an apparently solid wall which swung open like a gateway to freedom. In a revival of the production at the Royal Dramatic Theatre, Stockholm, in 1989, Bergman deployed many of the same devices, although Nora's final escape on this occasion was made through the auditorium, observed from the stage by her little daughter clutching a doll.

Other German productions of note have included a revival by Rudolf Noelte at Berlin's Renaissance-Theater, in 1976, and one by Peter Zadek at the Bremer Kammerspiele in Bremen, in 1967, with Edit Clever as Nora. Zadek opted for a minimalist form of staging which was designed to lay bare the play's essence and to enforce a sense of critical distance which produced an almost Brechtian-style 'alienation-effect'. What has also been characterised as the *shockstil* (shock-style) of this production might also have been said to have characterised Hans Neuenfels' production at the Stuttgart-Wurttemberg State Theatre in 1972, which stressed an anti-bourgeois element in its conception. The setting, by Klaus Gelhaar, seemed to reflect Helmer's dreams of grandeur in its green and white palatial lineaments, displacing the usual middle-class cosiness, and dominated by a huge set of rear windows hung with funereal drapes. The actors struck puppet-like poses and the play's ending was staged as a mixture of the absurd and the ironic as Nora ascended a ladder to effect an exit through the rear windows before reappearing, almost immediately, as an orphan-like face pressed to the glass as if seeking readmission from exposure to the wintry harshness of the world outside.

British productions

The first production of *A Doll's House* in Britain took place in 1884, based on a translation by Henrietta Frances Lord, who had an eccentric belief in a Christian version of Pythagoras's theory of the transmigration of souls. She entitled the play *Nora* and appended a preface in which she described the play in ways which amounted to its being little more than a tract for the twin causes of Feminism and Christian Science. Two years later a bowdlerised and expurgated version of this translation by Henry Arthur Jones and Henry Herman entitled *Breaking a Butterfly*, which both sentimentalised and melodramatised Ibsen's play, opened at the new Prince's Theatre in London. Not only did the adapters alter the ending but they also invented a number of new characters with English names, including four members of the 'Goddard' family, a 'Philip Dunkley' (played

by Herbert Beerbohm Tree) and two other characters called 'Martin
Grittle' and 'Dan Bradbury'. The play's ending had Helmer take
upon himself the blame for Nora's past indiscretions while Nora
herself concluded as a sweetly repentant wife and mother.

A famous amateur performance took place in 1886 in a private
drawing room in London's Bloomsbury district organised by Karl
Marx's daughter, Eleanor, who played Nora opposite her common-
law husband, Edward Aveling, who played Helmer. William Morris's
daughter, May, played Mrs Linde and no less a figure than the
young Bernard Shaw, who had already written his *Quintessence
of Ibsenism* two years earlier, played Krogstad. But the first
professional production of the play was given in London at the
Novelty Theatre in June 1889, directed by Charles Carrington, with
his wife, Janet Achurch, as Nora. Carrington himself played Helmer.
The production was planned to run for a week but lasted for three.
The translation was a distinguished one by William Archer, who
went on to translate most of Ibsen's plays into English. The critic
Clement Scott, who tended subsequently to be hostile to Ibsen and
who famously loathed *Ghosts*, admired Achurch's performance and
although the 'restlessness of the child wife in the first act was a trifle
forced [...] nothing could have been better than the scene with the
doctor [...] and the whole of her share in the last long duologue
was as good as it could be [...] The interest was so intense [...]
that a pin might have been heard to drop [...] and when the curtain
fell there was such cheering that Mr Carrington promised to
telegraph the happy result to Henrik Ibsen' (unsigned notice by
Scott in the *Daily Telegraph*, 8 June 1889, in Egan, 1972, pp. 102–3).
In an interview, Achurch described the strain of undertaking such a
large role which she considered 'heavier than Hamlet' (ibid. p. 124).
Not all criticism was positive, however; in fact the London press
was predominantly hostile, the play being described as 'morbid and
unwholesome' by *The Times*, while the ciritc of the *Sporting and
Dramatic News* declared that he 'had never sat out a play more
dreary or illogical as a whole, or in its details more feeble or
commonplace. It is as though someone had dramatized the cooking
of a Sunday dinner' (quoted in Michael Meyer ed., *File on Ibsen*,
London, Methuen, 1985, p. 35).

Attending a revival in 1892 at London's Avenue Theatre, again
with Janet Achurch, the trade-union leader John Burns noted in his
diary that the theatre had been 'half-filled with socialists' – an
indication as to how Ibsen was being interpreted at the time.
Achurch again performed the role at two London venues – the

Royalty Theatre in 1893 and, penultimately, in 1897 at the Globe
Theatre. Viewing this last, Shaw was struck less by the play's
political implications than by both Achurch's performance and that
of Courtney Thorpe as Helmer. The latter played the part with
passion. It is the first time we have seen this done; and the effect is
overwhelming. We no longer study an object lesson in lord-of-
creationism, appealing to our sociological interest only. We see a
fellow-creature blindly wrecking his happiness and losing his "love
life", and are touched dramatically' (Bernard Shaw, *Our Theatres in
the Nineties*, London, Constable, 1954, p. 132). As far as Achurch's
performance was concerned, she was 'far ahead of any living English
actress of her generation in this class of work' and, after discussing
the subtleties of her acting in some detail, Shaw concluded that
'Nora has all her old vitality and originality, and more than her old
hold on the audience, she is less girlish and more sophisticated with
the passions of the stage than she was at the Novelty when she first
captivated us' (ibid. pp. 132–3). Achurch's last performance of the
role was given at the Kingsway Theatre, London, in 1911.

The 1920s and 1930s saw London performances by Madge
Titheradge at the Playhouse Theatre in 1925, two performances by
Gwen Ffrangcon-Davies – at the Arts Theatre and the Criterion
Theatre, both in 1930 – and two performances of the role by Lydia
Lopokova – at the Arts Theatre in 1934 and at the Criterion Theatre
in 1936. James Agate, reviewing the 1930 Criterion production
bewailed the continued dominance in British Ibsen of 'the dingy
parlours hung with penitential gloom' and while praising Lopokova's
performance, criticised the ponderous reproduction of the drawing-
room milieu with its hideous stuffiness. Reviewing a production in
1939 at the Duke of York's Theatre, directed by Marius Goring, and
with Lucie Mannheim and Austin Trevor, Agate again had cause to
criticise the decor. Although he felt that Marius Goring had produced
'excitingly', he disapproved of 'the amazing architecture of Torvald's
summer palace, which appears to be on the ground floor of Park
Lane's latest and most luxurious block of flats'. Agate also thought
that 'Miss Lucie Mannheim's Nora should not be allowed to let off
shrieks and whistles which suggest a railway engine in hysteria',
although 'a great deal of her Nora is exceedingly touching, and the
end of the second act is very nearly the best I have seen'. He was
especially struck by the staging of Rank's final exit, 'in gala costume,
with confetti on his shoulders, and on his forehead a mask to which
is attached a balloon, baleful and ridiculous. It is as though Ibsen,
foreseeing Strindberg and wishful to take the wind out of his sails,

had thrown in an entire Strindberg play as a mere decoration' (James
Agate, *Red Letter Nights*, London, Jonathan Cape, 1944, pp. 60–2).

Peter Ashmore's 1953 revival at the Lyric, Hammersmith, starred
Mai Zetterling and Mogens Wieth in a setting which opened up the
entire living area of the Helmer apartment to include a bedroom,
where the final scene was played in such a manner as to stress the
sexual aspect of their eight-year relationship as an important
contributory factor in Nora's decision to leave. Patrick Garland
directed a notable production of the play at London's Criterion
Theatre in 1973, designed by John Bury and with Claire Bloom and
Colin Blakely. Bloom's performance was described as one of 'high
theatrical intelligence [...] you can see from the beginning every
bright-eyed, feverish, whimsical move has been laid to prepare for
the climax. [...] Miss Bloom [...] comes up with a credible
vulnerability, a genuine affection for her husband and a frantic
neurosis about her impending disgrace [and] emerges not as a
plaything but as someone on the brink of womanhood'. In this she
was matched by the 'intelligence and power' of Colin Blakely's
performance as Torvald in a play where 'husband, as well as wife, is
playing at parenthood and marriage. I'd guess that it was this double
exposure which gives the play's shock-waves their power' (Helen
Dawson in *Plays and Players*, March 1973, pp. 42–3).

Probably the finest of the more recent productions of *A Doll's
House* was the one directed by Adrian Noble, in the round, at the
Barbican Centre's intimate Pit Theatre in 1982, with Cheryl
Campbell as Nora. Michael Billington described the production as
achieving 'an almost holy intensity', in which 'the central dynamic
comes from Cheryl Campbell's extraordinary Nora', played as 'a
schizoid, suicidal near-hysteric', in such a way that 'the final
discovery of her real self becomes not merely moving but cleansing'.
The famous tarantella scene concluded with frenzied laughter and
wild cartwheels. Playing opposite her, Stephen Moore offered 'an
almost definitive Torvald: no paternalist villain but someone trapped
inside the role of the doll-husband'. The great strengths of the
director's interpretation stemmed from the fact that 'every character
is seen from his or her point of view' in a production that provided
'new perspectives on a great classic' (Michael Billington, *One Night
Stands*, London, Nick Hern Books, 1993, pp. 185–6).

Anthony Page staged what was described as a 'revelatory revival'
at the Playhouse Theatre, London, in 1996, with Janet McTeer and
Owen Teale. McTeer's performance was characterised as having
'greatness' in the way she contrived to wear her infantilism 'like a

disguise'. Teale's Welsh Torvald was a 'strapping, virile ox with a self-sentimentalising streak', a man who, 'if he were to kill or rape his wife, would blubber with fetching self-pity afterwards'. The critic's experience was genuinely cathartic and he urged his readers to 'go to see this compulsory account of a very great play' (Paul Taylor, *Independent*, 26 October 1996).

Other recent productions have included one at the Royal Lyceum Theatre, Edinburgh, in 1987 (with Judi Bowker), at the Palace Theatre, Watford, in 1987 (with Susan Penhaligon), at the Royal Exchange, Manchester, in 1987 (with Brenda Blethyn), at the Riverside Studios, London, in 2000 (with Anne-Marie Duff), and one by the Birmingham Repertory Theatre Company in 2004 (with Tara Fitzgerald). Some of these have assumed a more stylised approach, none more so than the productions by Lou Stein in Watford and the one given by the Shared Experience group at the New Ambassadors Theatre, London, in 2000. Both can be described as 'expressionist' in nature. The Watford production had decor by Stefanos Lazaridis, who provided a series of 'black Norwegian pine screens that steal about, revealing ominous figures [...] eerily lit' (Giles Gordon, *Evening Standard*, 2 November 1987). The impression was 'both womb-like and funereal, from an oppressive slanting ceiling to dark gleaming walls that slide apart' to reveal Nora, at the play's beginning 'spot-lit in stifling, all-enveloping blackness, stuffing into macaroons out of a paper bag'. This was a 'Lolita-like interpretation, adolescent puppy fat ripening into voluptuousness', with Nora's final bid for freedom signalled by 'flying the ceiling away as she hurls the sliding walls aside' (Martin Hoyle, *Financial Times*, 2 November 1987).

The less successful Shared Experience production cast a black actor, Paterson Joseph, as Helmer opposite the diminutive Anne-Marie Duff, who was first seen stuck in a literal doll's house which, like Alice in Wonderland, she had obviously outgrown. The figure of Krogstad remained onstage throughout like a threatening, beggarly presence, occasionally writhing at her feet, and the tarantella was performed with Nora clutching the doll's house roof. In addition to Krogstad's spectral presence, 'every time Nora mentions her father, Pip Donaghy appears dangling a bag of macaroons in front of her as if she were a domestic pet. [...] The intention is to remind us that Ibsen was not a purely naturalistic dramatist. But whoever supposed that he was?' (Michael Billington, *Guardian*, 1 November 2000).

Film versions

A 1922 screen version, with Alla Nazimova and Alan Hale, was
apparently the fifth silent film version of the play to be made in
America. It then seems to have fallen out of favour until later in the
century when Rainer Werner Fassbinder made a German video
version in 1973, which was wildely seen on European television.
According to Marker and Marker, 'In this heavily edited cinematic
de(con)struction of *A Doll's House*, the heroine – played by the
Fassbinder star Margit Carstensen – became a materialistic society
woman cynically intent on the acquisition of power and the selfish
preservation of her social and marital position. [. . .] Carstensen
depicted a timelessly bourgeois Hausfrau, fully as responsible as her
husband for their unhealthy marriage and for the power struggle it
has become' (op. cit., p. 77–8). Ingmar Bergman's film *Scenes from a
Marriage* (1973), which he also adapted for the stage, is said to have
been inspired by *A Doll's House*. Originally part of a six-part TV
series, it starred Liv Ullmann and Erland Josephson, with Bibi
Andersson as 'the other woman', and was shot largely in close-up in
order to emphasise the tensions between the protagonists.

In 1973 two other filmed versions of the play appeared – one
directed by Patrick Garland and based on his own stage production
with Claire Bloom; the other directed by Joseph Losey and starring
Jane Fonda. Both films had very strong casts. Claire Bloom's
performance gained support from Anthony Hopkins's Torvald, Ralph
Richardson's Dr Rank, Denholm Elliott's Krogstad and Anna
Massey's Mrs Linde, while no less a person than Dame Edith Evans
put in a cameo appearance as the nanny. The screenplay was by
British playwright, Christopher Hampton. Losey's film, which was
based on a screenplay by yet another British playwright, David
Mercer, had an all-star cast which, as well as Fonda, included David
Warner as Torvald, Trevor Howard as Dr Rank, Delphine Seyrig as
Mrs Linde and Edward Fox as Krogstad.

More recently, the British director, David Thacker, who had
staged *Ghosts* and Arthur Miller's version of *An Enemy of the
People* at London's Young Vic Theatre, made a TV version of *A
Doll's House* for the BBC in 1992, which was his first work for
television and highly praised. An excellent cast, which included Juliet
Stevenson, Trevor Eve, Geraldine James, David Calder and Patrick
Malahide, prospered under Thacker's 'enormously generous'
direction, where it was 'the warped pattern of relationships that is
unpicked [in what was] a depiction of real life, not a morality play'
(Nigella Lawson, *The Times*, 28 November 1992).

Further reading

Ibsen in English translation

All sixteen of Ibsen's plays, translated and introduced by Michael
Meyer, are collected in six paperbacks in Methuen Drama's World
Classics series. (1: *Ghosts, The Wild Duck, The Master Builder;* 2:
A Doll's House, An Enemy of the People, Hedda Gabler; 3:
Rosmersholm, The Lady from the Sea, Little Eyolf; 4: *The Pillars
of Society, John Gabriel Borkman, When We Dead Awaken;* 5:
Brand, Emperor and Galilean; 6: *Peer Gynt, The Pretenders.*)
Also available as Methuen Drama Student Editions: *Hedda Gabler*
and *Ghosts.*
The Oxford Ibsen. Volume 5 of this 8-volume series contains *Pillars
of Society, A Doll's House* and *Ghosts*, translated and edited by
James McFarlane. It also includes a selection of the dramatist's
draft material, accounts of early performances and extensive
bibliographical information.

Criticism

M.C. Bradbrook, *Ibsen the Norwegian: a Revaluation*, London,
Chatto and Windus, 1966. This critical study by an outstanding
scholar and writer on the theatre draws attention to the
specifically Norwegian qualities of Ibsen's work.
Errol Durbach, *'A Doll's House' – Ibsen's Myth of Transformation*,
Boston, Twayne, 1991.
Michael Egan (ed.), *Ibsen: the Critical Heritage*, London, Routledge
and Kegan Paul, 1972. Contains a wealth of interesting
contemporary reviews, articles, theatre notices, letters and critical
studies of the plays. Pages 101–23 are devoted to *A Doll's House.*
Robert Ferguson, *Henrik Ibsen: A New Biography*, Richard Cohen
Books, 1996. A highly readable biography which takes advantage
of earlier efforts in the field and manages to add some fresh
information.
Elizabeth Hardwick, 'Ibsen's Women' in E. Hardwick, *Seduction and
Betrayal: Women and Literature*, New York, Vintage Books, 1975.

Sally Ledger, *Henrik Ibsen*, Plymouth, Northcote House, 1999. This has good chapters on 'Ibsensim and *A Doll's House*' and 'Ibsen's Women'.

James McFarlane, *Henrik Ibsen. A Critical Anthology*, Penguin, 1970. A very useful volume in which the editor has selected passages written between 1881 and 1968 to cover the widest possible range of opinion and critical viewpoint. There are a large number of entries dealing with *Ghosts*.

James McFarlane, *The Cambridge Companion to Ibsen*, Cambridge, 1994. An excellent collection of essays edited by an outstanding Ibsen scholar and translator and covering just about every aspect of Ibsen's work. Essential reading.

J. Northam, *Ibsen's Dramatic Method: A Study of the Prose Dramas*, London, Faber, 1953. A tremendously important and influential book in which the author analyses Ibsen's theatrical technique in a most accessible and enlightening manner. Chapter I is on *A Doll's House*.

Yvonne Shafer (ed.), *Approaches to Teaching Ibsen's 'A Doll's House'*, New York, MLAA, 1985.

Joan Templeton, 'The Poetry of Feminism' in Joan Templeton (ed.), *Ibsen's Women*, Cambridge, CUP, 1997.

P.F.D. Tennant, *Ibsen's Dramatic Technique*, London, Bowes and Bowes, 1948. A slim, 120-page volume packed with insight and enthusiastically written. An excellent introduction to Ibsen's general approach to play making.

David Thomas, *Henrik Ibsen*, Basingstoke, Macmillan, 1983. A concise study of Ibsen's life and works. Chapter 4 deals with *A Doll's House* among other plays and Chapter 6 discusses specific points about Ibsen's plays in production.

Egil Törnquist, 'Representing the Source Text: Ibsen's *Et Dukkehjem/A Doll's House* (1879)', in Egil Törnquist, *Transposing Drama – Studies in Representation*, Basingstoke, Macmillan, 1991.

A Doll's House

Characters

TORVALD HELMER, *a lawyer*
NORA, *his wife*
DR. RANK
MRS. LINDE
NILS KROGSTAD, *also a lawyer*
NURSE, ANNE-MARIE
MAID, HELEN
THE HELMERS' THREE SMALL CHILDREN
A PORTER

The action takes place in the HELMERS' *apartment.*

ACT ONE

A comfortably and tastefully, but not expensively furnished room. Backstage right a door leads to the hall; backstage left, another door to HELMER's *study. Between these two doors stands a piano. In the middle of the left-hand wall is a door, with a window downstage of it. Near the window, a round table with armchairs and a small sofa. In the right-hand wall, slightly upstage, is a door; downstage of this, against the same wall, a stove lined with porcelain tiles, with a couple of armchairs and a rocking-chair in front of it. Between the stove and the side door is a small table. Engravings on the wall. A what-not with china and other bric-à-brac; a small bookcase with leather-bound books. A carpet on the floor; a fire in the stove. A winter day.*

> *A bell rings in the hall outside. After a moment we hear the front door being opened.* NORA *enters the room, humming contentedly to herself. She is wearing outdoor clothes and carrying a lot of parcels, which she puts down on the table right. She leaves the door to the hall open; through it, we can see a* PORTER *carrying a Christmas tree and a basket. He gives these to the* MAID, *who has opened the door for them.*

NORA. Hide that Christmas tree away, Helen. The children mustn't see it before I've decorated it this evening. (*To the* PORTER, *taking out her purse*) How much – ?
PORTER. A shilling.
NORA. Here's a pound. No, keep it. generous

> *The* PORTER *touches his cap and goes.* NORA *closes the door. She continues to laugh happily to herself as she removes her coat, etc. She takes from her pocket a bag containing macaroons and eats a couple. Then she tiptoes across and listens at her husband's door.*

NORA. Yes, he's here. (*Starts humming again as she goes over to the table, right.*)

HELMER (*from his room*). Is that my skylark twittering out there?

NORA (*opening some of the parcels*). It is!

HELMER. Is that my squirrel rustling?

NORA. Yes!

HELMER. When did my squirrel come home?

NORA. Just now. (*Pops the bag of macaroons in her pocket and wipes her mouth.*) Come out here, Torvald, and see what I've bought.

HELMER. You mustn't disturb me!

Short pause; then he opens the door and looks in, his pen in his hand.

HELMER. Bought, did you say? All that? Has my little squander-bird been overspending again?

NORA. Oh, Torvald, surely we can let ourselves go a little this year! It's the first Christmas we don't have to scrape.

HELMER. Well, you know, we can't afford to be extravagant.

NORA. Oh yes, Torvald, we can be a little extravagant now. Can't we? Just a tiny bit? You've got a big salary now, and you're going to make lots and lots of money.

HELMER. Next year, yes. But my new salary doesn't start till April.

NORA. Pooh; we can borrow till then.

HELMER. Nora! (*Goes over to her and takes her playfully by the ear.*) What a little spendthrift you are! Suppose I were to borrow fifty pounds today, and you spent it all over Christmas, and then on New Year's Eve a tile fell off a roof on to my head –

NORA (*puts her hand over his mouth*). Oh, Torvald! Don't say such dreadful things!

HELMER. Yes, but suppose something like that did happen? What then?

NORA. If anything as frightful as that happened, it wouldn't make much difference whether I was in debt or not.

HELMER. But what about the people I'd borrowed from?

NORA. Them? Who cares about them? They're strangers. *innocent*

HELMER. Oh, Nora, Nora, how like a woman! No, but seriously, Nora, you know how I feel about this. No debts! Never borrow! *sensible* A home that is founded on debts and borrowing can never be a place of freedom and beauty. We two have stuck it out bravely up to now; and we shall continue to do so for the few weeks that remain.

NORA (*goes over towards the stove*). Very well, Torvald. As you say.

HELMER (*follows her*). Now, now! My little songbird mustn't droop her wings. What's this? Is little squirrel sulking? (*Takes out his purse.*) Nora; guess what I've got here! *playful.*

NORA (*turns quickly*). Money!

HELMER. Look. (*Hands her some banknotes.*) I know how these small expenses crop up at Christmas.

NORA (*counts them*). One – two – three – four. Oh, thank you, Torvald, thank you! I should be able to manage with this.

HELMER. You'll have to.

NORA. Yes, yes, of course I will. But come over here, I want to show you everything I've bought. And so cheap! Look, here are new clothes for Ivar – and a sword. And a horse and a trumpet for Bob. And a doll and a cradle for Emmy – they're nothing much, but she'll pull them apart in a few days. And some bits of material and handkerchiefs for the maids. Old Anne-Marie ought to have had something better, really.

HELMER. And what's in that parcel?

NORA (*cries*). No, Torvald, you mustn't see that before this evening!

HELMER. Very well. But now, tell me, my little spendthrift, what do you want for Christmas?

NORA. Me? Oh, pooh, I don't want anything.

HELMER. Oh yes, you do. Now tell me, what within reason would you most like?

NORA. No, I really don't know. Oh, yes – Torvald – !

HELMER. Well?

NORA (*plays with his coat-buttons; not looking at him*). If you really want to give me something, you could – you could –

HELMER. Come on, out with it.

NORA (*quickly*). You could give me money, Torvald. Only as much as you feel you can afford; then later I'll buy something with it.

HELMER. But, Nora –

NORA. Oh yes, Torvald dear, please! Please! Then I'll wrap up the notes in pretty gold paper and hang them on the Christmas tree. Wouldn't that be fun?

HELMER. What's the name of that little bird that can never keep any money?

NORA. Yes, yes, squanderbird; I know. But let's do as I say, Torvald; then I'll have time to think about what I need most. Isn't that the best way? Mm?

HELMER (*smiles*). To be sure it would be, if you could keep what I give you and really buy yourself something with it. But you'll spend it on all sorts of useless things for the house, and then I'll have to put my hand in my pocket again.

NORA. Oh, but Torvald –

HELMER. You can't deny it, Nora dear. (*Puts his arm around her waist.*) The squanderbird's a pretty little creature, but she gets through an awful lot of money. It's incredible what an expensive pet she is for a man to keep.

NORA. For shame! How can you say such a thing? I save every penny I can.

HELMER (*laughs*). That's quite true. Every penny you can. But you can't.

NORA (*hums and smiles, quietly gleeful*). Hm. If you only knew how many expenses we larks and squirrels have, Torvald.

HELMER. You're a funny little creature. Just like your father used to be. Always on the look-out for some way to get money, but as soon as you have any it just runs through your fingers and you never know where it's gone. Well, I suppose I must take you as you are. It's in your blood. Yes, yes, yes, these things are hereditary, Nora.

NORA. Oh, I wish I'd inherited more of papa's qualities.

HELMER. And I wouldn't wish my darling little songbird to be any different from what she is. By the way, that reminds me. You look awfully – how shall I put it? – awfully guilty today.

NORA. Do I?

HELMER. Yes, you do. Look me in the eyes.

NORA (*looks at him*). Well?

HELMER (*wags his finger*). Has my little sweet-tooth been indulging herself in town today, by any chance?

NORA. No, how can you think such a thing?

HELMER. Not a tiny little digression into a pastry shop?

NORA. No, Torvald, I promise –

HELMER. Not just a wee jam tart?

NORA. Certainly not.

HELMER. Not a little nibble at a macaroon?

NORA. No, Torvald – I promise you, honestly – !

HELMER. There, there. I was only joking.

NORA (*goes over to the table, right*). You know I could never act against your wishes.

HELMER. Of course not. And you've given me your word – (*Goes over to her.*) Well, my beloved Nora, you keep your little Christmas secrets to yourself. They'll be revealed this evening, I've no doubt, once the Christmas tree has been lit.

NORA. Have you remembered to invite Dr Rank?

HELMER. No. But there's no need; he knows he'll be dining with us. Anyway, I'll ask him when he comes this morning. I've ordered some good wine. Oh, Nora, you can't imagine how I'm looking forward to this evening.

NORA. So am I. And, Torvald, how the children will love it!

HELMER. Yes, it's a wonderful thing to know that one's position is assured and that one has an ample income. Don't you agree? It's good to know that, isn't it?

NORA. Yes, it's almost like a miracle.

HELMER. Do you remember last Christmas? For three whole weeks you shut yourself away every evening to make flowers for the Christmas tree, and all those other things you were going to surprise us with. Ugh, it was the most boring time I've ever had in my life.

NORA. I didn't find it boring.

HELMER (*smiles*). But it all came to nothing in the end, didn't it?

NORA. Oh, are you going to bring that up again? How could I help the cat getting in and tearing everything to bits?

HELMER. No, my poor little Nora, of course you couldn't. You simply wanted to make us happy, and that's all that matters. But it's good that those hard times are past.

NORA. Yes, it's wonderful.

HELMER. I don't have to sit by myself and be bored. And you don't have to tire your pretty eyes and your delicate little hands –

NORA (*claps her hands*). No, Torvald, that's true, isn't it? I don't have to any longer! Oh, it's really all just like a miracle. (*Takes his arm.*) Now I'm going to tell you what I thought we might do, Torvald. As soon as Christmas is over –

A bell rings in the hall.

Oh, there's the doorbell. (*Tidies up one or two things in the room.*) Someone's coming. What a bore.

HELMER. I'm not at home to any visitors. Remember!

MAID (*in the doorway*). A lady's called, madam. A stranger.

NORA. Well, ask her to come in.

MAID. And the doctor's here too, sir.

HELMER. Has he gone to my room?

MAID. Yes, sir.

HELMER goes into his room. The MAID shows in MRS LINDE, who is dressed in travelling clothes; then closes the door.

MRS LINDE (*shyly and a little hesitantly*). Good morning, Nora.

NORA. (*uncertainly*). Good morning –

MRS LINDE. I don't suppose you recognize me.

NORA. No, I'm afraid I – Yes, wait a minute – surely – ! (*Exclaims.*) Why, Christine! Is it really you?

MRS LINDE. Yes, it's me.

NORA. Christine! And I didn't recognize you! But how could I – ? (*More quietly.*) How you've changed, Christine!

MRS LINDE. Yes, I know. It's been nine years – nearly ten –

NORA. Is it so long? Yes, it must be. Oh, these last eight years have been such a happy time for me! So you've come to town? All that way in winter! How brave of you!

MRS LINDE. I arrived by the steamer this morning.

NORA. Yes, of course, to enjoy yourself over Christmas. Oh, how splendid! We'll have to celebrate! But take off your coat. You're not cold, are you? (*Helps her off with it.*) There! Now let's sit down here by the stove and be comfortable. No, you take the armchair. I'll sit here in the rocking-chair. (*Clasps* MRS LINDE's *hands.*) Yes, now you look like your old self. Just at first I – you've got a little paler, though, Christine. And perhaps a bit thinner.

MRS LINDE. And older, Nora. Much, much older.

NORA. Yes, perhaps a little older. Just a tiny bit. Not much. (*Checks herself suddenly and says earnestly.*) Oh, but how thoughtless of me to sit here and chatter away like this! Dear, sweet Christine, can you forgive me?

MRS LINDE. What do you mean, Nora?

NORA (*quietly*). Poor Christine, you've become a widow.

MRS LINDE. Yes. Three years ago.

NORA. I know, I know — I read it in the papers. Oh, Christine, I meant to write to you so often, honestly. But I always put it off, and something else always cropped up.

MRS LINDE. I understand, Nora dear.

NORA. No, Christine, it was beastly of me. Oh, my poor darling, what you've gone through! And he didn't leave you anything?

MRS LINDE. No.

NORA. No children, either?

MRS LINDE. No.

NORA. Nothing at all, then?

MRS LINDE. Not even a feeling of loss or sorrow.

NORA (*looks incredulously at her.*) But, Christine, how is that possible?

MRS LINDE (*smiles sadly and strokes* NORA's *hair*). Oh, these things happen, Nora.

NORA. All alone. How dreadful that must be for you. I've three lovely children. I'm afraid you can't see them now, because they're out with Nanny. But you must tell me everything –

MRS LINDE. No, no, no. I want to hear about you.

NORA. No, you start. I'm not going to be selfish today, I'm just going to think about you. Oh, but there's one thing I *must* tell you. Have you heard of the wonderful luck we've just had?

MRS LINDE. No. What?

NORA. Would you believe it – my husband's just been made vice-president of the bank!

MRS LINDE. Your husband? Oh, how lucky – !

NORA. Yes, isn't it? Being a lawyer is so uncertain, you know, especially if one isn't prepared to touch any case that isn't – well – quite nice. And of course Torvald's been very firm about that – and I'm absolutely with him. Oh, you can imagine how happy we are! He's joining the bank in the New Year, and he'll be getting a big salary, and lots of percentages too. From now on we'll be able to live quite differently – we'll be able to do whatever we want. Oh, Christine, it's such a relief! I feel so happy! Well, I mean, it's lovely to have heaps of money and not to have to worry about anything. Don't you think?

MRS LINDE. It must be lovely to have enough to cover one's needs, anyway.

NORA. Not just our needs! We're going to have heaps and heaps of money!

MRS LINDE (*smiles*). Nora, Nora, haven't you grown up yet? When we were at school you were a terrible little spendthrift.

NORA (*laughs quietly*). Yes, Torvald still says that. (*Wags her finger.*) But 'Nora, Nora' isn't as silly as you think. Oh, we've

been in no position for me to waste money. We've both had to
work.

MRS LINDE. You too?

NORA. Yes, little things – fancy work, crocheting, embroidery
and so forth. (*Casually.*) And other things too. I suppose you
know Torvald left the Ministry when we got married? There
were no prospects of promotion in his department, and of
course he needed more money. But the first year he overworked himself dreadfully. He had to take on all sorts of extra
jobs, and worked day and night. But it was too much for him,
and he became frightfully ill. The doctors said he'd have to go
to a warmer climate.

MRS LINDE. Yes, you spent a whole year in Italy, didn't you?

NORA. Yes. It wasn't easy for me to get away, you know. I'd just
had Ivar. But, of course, we had to do it. Oh, it was a marvellous
trip! And it saved Torvald's life. But it cost an awful lot of
money, Christine.

MRS LINDE. I can imagine.

NORA. Two hundred and fifty pounds. That's a lot of money,
you know.

MRS LINDE. How lucky you had it.

NORA. Well, actually, we got it from my father.

MRS LINDE. Oh, I see. Didn't he die just about that time?

NORA. Yes, Christine, just about then. Wasn't it dreadful, I
couldn't go and look after him. I was expecting little Ivar any
day. And then I had my poor Torvald to care for – we really
didn't think he'd live. Dear, kind papa! I never saw him again,
Christine. Oh, it's the saddest thing that's happened to me
since I got married.

MRS LINDE. I know you were very fond of him. But you went
to Italy – ?

NORA. Yes. Well, we had the money, you see, and the doctors
said we mustn't delay. So we went the month after papa died.

MRS LINDE. And your husband came back completely cured?

NORA. Fit as a fiddle!

MRS LINDE. But – the doctor?

NORA. How do you mean?

MRS LINDE. I thought the maid said that the gentleman who arrived with me was the doctor.

NORA. Oh yes, that's Dr Rank, but he doesn't come because anyone's ill. He's our best friend, and he looks us up at least once every day. No, Torvald hasn't had a moment's illness since we went away. And the children are fit and healthy and so am I. (*Jumps up and claps her hands.*) Oh, God, oh God, Christine, isn't it a wonderful thing to be alive and happy! Oh, but how beastly of me! I'm only talking about myself. (*Sits on a footstool and rests her arms on* MRS LINDE's *knee.*) Oh, please don't be angry with me! Tell me, is it really true you didn't love your husband? Why did you marry him, then?

MRS LINDE. Well, my mother was still alive; and she was helpless and bedridden. And I had my two little brothers to take care of. I didn't feel I could say no.

NORA. Yes, well, perhaps you're right. He was rich then, was he?

MRS LINDE. Quite comfortably off, I believe. But his business was unsound, you see, Nora. When he died it went bankrupt and there was nothing left.

NORA. What did you do?

MRS LINDE. Well, I had to try to make ends meet somehow, so I started a little shop, and a little school, and anything else I could turn my hand to. These last three years have been just one endless slog for me, without a moment's rest. But now it's over, Nora. My poor dead mother doesn't need me any more; she's passed away. And the boys don't need me either; they've got jobs now and can look after themselves.

NORA. How relieved you must feel –

MRS LINDE. No, Nora. Just unspeakably empty. No one to live for any more. (*Gets up restlessly.*) That's why I couldn't bear to stay out there any longer, cut off from the world. I thought it'd be easier to find some work here that will exercise and occupy my mind. If only I could get a regular job – office work of some kind –

NORA. Oh but, Christine, that's dreadfully exhausting; and you look practically finished already. It'd be much better for you if you could go away somewhere.

MRS LINDE (*goes over to the window*). I have no pappa to pay for my holidays, Nora.

NORA (*gets up*). Oh, please don't be angry with me.

MRS LINDE. My dear Nora, it's I who should ask you not to be angry. That's the worst thing about this kind of situation – it makes one so bitter. One has no one to work for; and yet one has to be continually sponging for jobs. One has to live; and so one becomes completely egocentric. When you told me about this luck you've just had with Torvald's new job – can you imagine? – I was happy not so much on your account, as on my own.

NORA. How do you mean? Oh, I understand. You mean Torvald might be able to do something for you?

MRS LINDE. Yes, I was thinking that.

NORA. He will too, Christine. Just you leave it to me. I'll lead up to it so delicately, so delicately; I'll get him in the right mood. Oh, Christine, I do so want to help you.

MRS LINDE. It's sweet of you to bother so much about me, Nora. Especially since you know so little of the worries and hardships of life.

NORA. I? You say *I* know little of – ?

MRS LINDE (*smiles*). Well, good heavens – those bits of fancy-work of yours – well, really! You're a child, Nora.

NORA (*tosses her head and walks across the room*). You shouldn't say that so patronizingly.

MRS LINDE. Oh?

NORA. You're like the rest. You all think I'm incapable of getting down to anything serious –

MRS LINDE. My dear –

NORA. You think I've never had any worries like the rest of you.

MRS LINDE. Nora dear, you've just told me about all your difficulties –

NORA. Pooh – that! (*Quietly.*) I haven't told you about the big thing.

MRS LINDE. What big thing? What do you mean?

NORA. You patronize me, Christine; but you shouldn't. You're proud that you've worked so long and so hard for your mother.

MRS LINDE. I don't patronize anyone, Nora. But you're right – I am both proud and happy that I was able to make my mother's last months on earth comparatively easy.

NORA. And you're also proud at what you've done for your brothers.

MRS LINDE. I think I have a right to be.

NORA. I think so too. But let me tell you something, Christine. I too have done something to be proud and happy about.

MRS LINDE. I don't doubt it. But – how do you mean?

NORA. Speak quietly! Suppose Torvald should hear! He mustn't, at any price – no one must know, Christine – no one but you.

MRS LINDE. But what is this?

NORA. Come over here. (*Pulls her down on to the sofa beside her.*) Yes, Christine – I too have done something to be happy and proud about. It was I who saved Torvald's life.

MRS LINDE. Saved his – ? How did you save it?

NORA. I told you about our trip to Italy. Torvald couldn't have lived if he hadn't managed to get down there –

MRS LINDE. Yes, well – your father provided the money –

NORA (*smiles*). So Torvald and everyone else thinks. But –

MRS LINDE. Yes?

NORA. Papa didn't give us a penny. It was I who found the money.

MRS LINDE. You? All of it?

NORA. Two hundred and fifty pounds. What do you say to that?

MRS LINDE. But, Nora, how could you? Did you win a lottery or something?

NORA (*scornfully*). Lottery? (*Sniffs.*) What would there be to be proud of in that?

MRS LINDE. But where did you get it from, then?

NORA (*hums and smiles secretively*). Hm; tra-la-la-la!

MRS LINDE. You couldn't have borrowed it.

NORA. Oh? Why not?

MRS LINDE. Well, a wife can't borrow money without her husband's consent.

NORA (*tosses her head*). Ah, but when a wife has a little business sense, and knows how to be clever –

MRS LINDE. But Nora, I simply don't understand –

NORA. You don't have to. No one has said I borrowed the money. I could have got it in some other way. (*Throws herself back on the sofa.*) I could have got it from an admirer. When a girl's as pretty as I am –

MRS LINDE. Nora, you're crazy!

NORA. You're dying of curiosity now, aren't you, Christine?

MRS LINDE. Nora dear, you haven't done anything foolish?

NORA (*sits up again*). Is it foolish to save one's husband's life?

MRS LINDE. I think it's foolish if without his knowledge you –

NORA. But the whole point was that he mustn't know! Great heavens, don't you see? He hadn't to know how dangerously ill he was. It was me they told that his life was in danger and that only going to a warm climate could save him. Do you suppose I didn't try to think of other ways of getting him down there? I told him how wonderful it would be for me to go abroad like other young wives; I cried and prayed; I asked him to remember my condition, and said he ought to be nice and tender to me; and then I suggested he might quite easily borrow the money. But then he got almost angry with me, Christine. He said I was frivolous, and that it was his duty as a husband not to pander to my moods and caprices – I think

that's what he called them. Well, well, I thought, you've got to
be saved somehow. And then I thought of a way –

MRS LINDE. But didn't your husband find out from your father
that the money hadn't come from him?

NORA. No, never. Papa died just then. I'd thought of letting
him into the plot and asking him not to tell. But since he was so
ill – ! And as things turned out, it didn't become necessary.

MRS LINDE. And you've never told your husband about this?

NORA. For heaven's sake, no! What an idea! He's frightfully
strict about such matters. And besides – he's so proud of being
a man – it'd be so painful and humiliating for him to know that
he owed anything to me. It'd completely wreck our relationship.
This life we have built together would no longer exist.

MRS LINDE. Will you never tell him?

NORA (*thoughtfully, half-smiling*). Yes – some time, perhaps. Years
from now, when I'm no longer pretty. You mustn't laugh! I
mean, of course, when Torvald no longer loves me as he does
now; when it no longer amuses him to see me dance and dress
up and play the fool for him. Then it might be useful to have
something up my sleeve. (*Breaks off.*) Stupid, stupid, stupid!
That time will never come. Well, what do you think of my big
secret, Christine? I'm not completely useless, am I? Mind
you, all this has caused me a frightful lot of worry. It hasn't
been easy for me to meet my obligations punctually. In case
you don't know, in the world of business there are things called
quarterly instalments and interest, and they're a terrible problem to cope with. So I've had to scrape a little here and save a
little there, as best I can. I haven't been able to save much on the
housekeeping money, because Torvald likes to live well; and I
couldn't let the children go short of clothes – I couldn't take
anything out of what he gives me for them. The poor little
angels!

MRS LINDE. So you've had to stint yourself, my poor Nora?

NORA. Of course. Well, after all, it was my problem. Whenever
Torvald gave me money to buy myself new clothes, I never

used more than half of it; and I always bought what was cheapest and plainest. Thank heaven anything suits me, so that Torvald's never noticed. But it made me a bit sad sometimes, because it's lovely to wear pretty clothes. Don't you think?

MRS LINDE. Indeed it is.

NORA. And then I've found one or two other sources of income. Last winter I managed to get a lot of copying to do. So I shut myself away and wrote every evening, late into the night. Oh, I often got so tired, so tired. But it was great fun, though, sitting there working and earning money. It was almost like being a man.

MRS LINDE. But how much have you managed to pay off like this?

NORA. Well, I can't say exactly. It's awfully difficult to keep an exact check on these kind of transactions. I only know I've paid everything I've managed to scrape together. Sometimes I really didn't know where to turn. (*Smiles.*) Then I'd sit here and imagine some rich old gentleman had fallen in love with me –

MRS LINDE. What! What gentleman?

NORA. Silly! And that now he'd died and when they opened his will it said in big letters: 'Everything I possess is to be paid forthwith to my beloved Mrs Nora Helmer in cash.'

MRS LINDE. But, Nora dear, who was this gentleman?

NORA. Great heavens, don't you understand? There wasn't any old gentleman; he was just something I used to dream up as I sat here evening after evening wondering how on earth I could raise some money. But what does it matter? The old bore can stay imaginary as far as I'm concerned, because now I don't have to worry any longer! (*Jumps up.*) Oh, Christine, isn't it wonderful? I don't have to worry any more! No more troubles! I can play all day with the children, I can fill the house with pretty things, just the way Torvald likes. And, Christine, it'll soon be spring, and the air'll be fresh and the skies blue – and then perhaps we'll be able to take a little trip somewhere. I shall

be able to see the sea again. Oh, yes, yes, it's a wonderful thing
to be alive and happy!

The bell rings in the hall.

MRS LINDE (*gets up*). You've a visitor. Perhaps I'd better go.

NORA. No, stay. It won't be for me. It's someone for Torvald –

MAID (*in the doorway*). Excuse me, madam, a gentleman's called
who says he wants to speak to the master. But I didn't know –
seeing as the doctor's with him –

NORA. Who is this gentleman?

KROGSTAD (*in the doorway*). It's me, Mrs Helmer.

MRS LINDE *starts, composes herself and turns away to the
window.*

NORA (*takes a step towards him and whispers tensely*). You? What
is it? What do you want to talk to my husband about?

KROGSTAD. Business – you might call it. I hold a minor post in
the bank, and I hear your husband is to become our new chief –

NORA. Oh – then it isn't – ?

KROGSTAD. Pure business, Mrs Helmer. Nothing more.

NORA. Well, you'll find him in his study.

*Nods indifferently as she closes the hall door behind him. Then
she walks across the room and sees to the stove.*

MRS LINDE. Nora, who was that man?

NORA. A lawyer called Krogstad.

MRS LINDE. It was him, then.

NORA. Do you know that man?

MRS LINDE. I used to know him – some years ago. He was a
solicitor's clerk in our town, for a while.

NORA. Yes, of course, so he was.

MRS LINDE. How he's changed!

NORA. He was very unhappily married, I believe.

MRS LINDE. Is he a widower now?

NORA. Yes, with a lot of children. Ah, now it's alight.

*She closes the door of the stove and moves the rocking-chair a
little to one side.*

MRS LINDE. He does – various things now, I hear?

NORA. Does he? It's quite possible I really don't know. But
   don't let's talk about business. It's so boring.

   DR RANK *enters from* HELMER's *study.*

DR RANK (*still in the doorway*). No, no, my dear chap, don't see
   me out. I'll go and have a word with your wife. (*Closes the door
   and notices* MRS LINDE.) Oh, I beg your pardon. I seem to be
   de trop here too.

NORA. Not in the least. (*Introduces them.*) Dr Rank. Mrs Linde.

RANK. Ah! A name I have often heard in this house. I believe I
   passed you on the stairs as I came up.

MRS LINDE. Yes. Stairs tire me. I have to take them slowly.

RANK. Oh, have you hurt yourself?

MRS LINDE. No, I'm just a little run down.

RANK. Ah, is that all? Then I take it you've come to town to cure
   yourself by a round of parties?

MRS LINDE. I have come here to find work.

RANK. Is that an approved remedy for being run down?

MRS LINDE. One has to live, Doctor.

RANK. Yes, people do seem to regard it as a necessity.

NORA. Oh, really, Dr Rank. I bet you want to stay alive.

RANK. You bet I do. However wretched I sometimes feel, I still
   want to go on being tortured for as long as possible. It's the
   same with all my patients; and with people who are morally
   sick, too. There's a moral cripple in with Helmer at this very
   moment –

MRS LINDE (*softly*). Oh!

NORA. Whom do you mean?

RANK. Oh, a lawyer fellow called Krogstad – you wouldn't know
   him. He's crippled all right; morally twisted. But even he started
   off by announcing, as though it were a matter of enormous
   importance, that he had to live.

NORA. Oh? What did he want to talk to Torvald about?

RANK. I haven't the faintest idea. All I heard was something
   about the bank.

NORA. I didn't know that Krog – that this man Krogstad had any connection with the bank.

RANK. Yes, he's got some kind of job down there. (*To* MRS LINDE.) I wonder if in your part of the world you too have a species of creature that spends its time fussing around trying to smell out moral corruption? And when they find a case they give him some nice, comfortable position so that they can keep a good watch on him. The healthy ones just have to lump it.

MRS LINDE. But surely it's the sick who need care most?

RANK (*shrugs his shoulders*). Well, there we have it. It's that attitude that's turning human society into a hospital.

NORA, *lost in her own thoughts, laughs half to herself and claps her hands*

RANK. Why are you laughing? Do you really know what society is?

NORA. What do I care about society? I think it's a bore. I was laughing at something else – something frightfully funny. Tell me, Dr Rank – will everyone who works at the bank come under Torvald now?

RANK. Do you find that particularly funny?

NORA (*smiles and hums*). Never you mind! Never you mind! (*Walks around the room.*) Yes, I find it very amusing to think that we – I mean, Torvald – has obtained so much influence over so many people. (*Takes the paper bag from her pocket.*) Dr Rank, would you like a small macaroon?

RANK. Macaroons! I say! I thought they were forbidden here.

NORA. Yes, well, these are some Christine gave me.

MRS LINDE. What? I – ?

NORA. All right, all right, don't get frightened. You weren't to know Torvald had forbidden them. He's afraid they'll ruin my teeth. But, dash it – for once – ! Don't you agree, Dr Rank? Here! (*Pops a macaroon into his mouth.*) You too, Christine. And I'll have one too. Just a little one. Two at the most (*Begins to walk round again.*) Yes, now I feel really, really happy. Now there's just one thing in the world I'd really love to do.

RANK. Oh? And what is that?

NORA. Just something I'd love to say to Torvald.

RANK. Well, why don't you say it?

NORA. No, I daren't. It's too dreadful.

MRS LINDE. Dreadful?

RANK. Well then, you'd better not. But you can say it to us. What is it you'd so love to say to Torvald?

NORA. I've the most extraordinary longing to say: 'Bloody hell!'

RANK. Are you mad?

MRS LINDE. My dear Nora – !

RANK. Say it. Here he is.

NORA (*hiding the bag of macaroons*). Ssh! Ssh!

    HELMER, *with his overcoat on his arm and his hat in his hand, enters from his study.*

NORA (*goes to meet him*). Well, Torvald dear, did you get rid of him?

HELMER. Yes, he's just gone.

NORA. May I introduce you – ? This is Christine. She's just arrived in town.

HELMER. Christine – ? Forgive me, but I don't think –

NORA. Mrs Linde, Torvald dear. Christine Linde.

HELMER. Ah. A childhood friend of my wife's, I presume?

MRS LINDE. Yes, we knew each other in earlier days.

NORA. And imagine, now she's travelled all this way to talk to you.

HELMER. Oh?

MRS LINDE. Well, I didn't really –

NORA. You see, Christine's frightfully good at office work, and she's mad to come under some really clever man who can teach her even more than she knows already –

HELMER. Very sensible, madam.

NORA. So when she heard you'd become head of the bank – it was in her local paper – she came here as quickly as she could and – Torvald, you will, won't you? Do a little something to help Christine? For my sake?

HELMER. Well, that shouldn't be impossible. You are a widow, I take it, Mrs Linde?

MRS LINDE. Yes.

HELMER. And you have experience of office work?

MRS LINDE. Yes, quite a bit.

HELMER. Well then, it's quite likely I may be able to find some job for you –

NORA (*claps her hands*). You see, you see!

HELMER. You've come at a lucky moment, Mrs Linde.

MRS LINDE. Oh, how can I ever thank you – ?

HELMER. There's absolutely no need. (*Puts on his overcoat.*) But now I'm afraid I must ask you to excuse me –

RANK. Wait. I'll come with you.

He gets his fur coat from the hall and warms it at the stove.

NORA. Don't be long, Torvald dear.

HELMER. I'll only be an hour.

NORA. Are you going too, Christine?

MRS LINDE (*puts on her outdoor clothes*). Yes, I must start to look round for a room.

HELMER. Then perhaps we can walk part of the way together.

NORA (*helps her*). It's such a nuisance we're so cramped here – I'm afraid we can't offer to –

MRS LINDE. Oh, I wouldn't dream of it. Goodbye, Nora dear, and thanks for everything.

NORA. *Au revoir.* You'll be coming back this evening, of course. And you too, Dr Rank. What? If you're well enough? Of course you'll be well enough. Wrap up warmly, though.

They go out, talking, into the hall. Children's voices are heard from the stairs.

NORA. Here they are! Here they are!

She runs out and opens the door. The NURSE, ANNE-MARIE, *enters with the children.*

NORA. Come in, come in! (*Stoops down and kisses them.*) Oh, my sweet darlings – ? Look at them, Christine! Aren't they beautiful?

RANK. Don't stand here chattering in this draught!

HELMER. Come, Mrs Linde. This is for mothers only.

DR RANK, HELMER and MRS LINDE go down the stairs. The NURSE brings the children into the room. NORA follows, and closes the door to the hall.

NORA. How well you look! What red cheeks you've got! Like apples and roses!

The CHILDREN answer her inaudibly as she talks to them.

NORA. Have you had fun? That's splendid. You gave Emmy and Bob a ride on the sledge? What, both together? I say! What a clever boy you are, Ivar! Oh, let me hold her for a moment Anne-Marie! My sweet little baby doll! (*Takes the smallest child from the NURSE and dances with her.*) Yes, yes, mummy will dance with Bob too. What? Have you been throwing snowballs? Oh, I wish I'd been there! No, don't – I'll undress them myself, Anne-Marie. No, please let me; it's such fun. Go inside and warm yourself; you look frozen. There's some hot coffee on the stove.

The NURSE goes into the room on the left. NORA takes off the children's outdoor clothes and throws them anywhere while they all chatter simultaneously.

NORA. What? A big dog ran after you? But he didn't bite you? No, dogs don't bite lovely little baby dolls. Leave those parcels alone, Ivar. What's in them? Ah, wouldn't you like to know! No, no; it's nothing nice. Come on, let's play a game. What shall we play? Hide and seek? Yes, let's play hide and seek. Bob shall hide first. You want me to? All right, let me hide first.

NORA and the CHILDREN play around the room, and in the adjacent room to the right, laughing and shouting. At length NORA hides under the table. The CHILDREN rush in, look, but cannot find her. Then they hear her half-stifled laughter, run to the table, lift up the cloth and see her. Great excitement. She crawls out as though to frighten them. Further excitement. Mean-

while, there has been a knock on the door leading from the hall, but no one has noticed it. Now the door is half opened and KROG-STAD *enters. He waits for a moment; the game continues.*

KROGSTAD. Excuse me, Mrs Helmer –

NORA (*turns with a stifled cry and half jumps up*). Oh! What do you want?

KROGSTAD. I beg your pardon – the front door was ajar. Someone must have forgotten to close it.

NORA (*gets up*). My husband is not at home, Mr Krogstad.

KROGSTAD. I know.

NORA. Well, what do you want here, then?

KROGSTAD. A word with you.

NORA. With – ? (*To the* CHILDREN, *quietly*.) Go inside to Anne-Marie. What? No, the strange gentleman won't do anything to hurt mummy. When he's gone we'll start playing again.

She takes the children into the room on the left and closes the door behind them.

NORA (*uneasy, tense*). You want to speak to me?

KROGSTAD. Yes.

NORA. Today? But it's not the first of the month yet.

KROGSTAD. No, it is Christmas Eve. Whether or not you have a merry Christmas depends on you.

NORA. What do you want? I can't give you anything today –

KROGSTAD. We won't talk about that for the present. There's something else. You have a moment to spare?

NORA. Oh, yes. Yes, I suppose so – though –

KROGSTAD. Good, I was sitting in the café down below and I saw your husband cross the street –

NORA. Yes.

KROGSTAD. With a lady.

NORA. Well?

KROGSTAD. Might I be so bold as to ask; was not that lady a Mrs Linde?

NORA. Yes.

KROGSTAD. Recently arrived in town?

NORA. Yes, today.

KROGSTAD. She is a good friend of yours, is she not?

NORA. Yes, she is. But I don't see –

KROGSTAD. I used to know her, too, once.

NORA. I know.

KROGSTAD. Oh? You've discovered that. Yes, I thought you would. Well then, may I ask you a straight question: is Mrs Linde to be employed at the bank?

NORA. How dare you presume to cross-examine me, Mr Krogstad? You, one of my husband's employees? But since you ask, you shall have an answer. Yes, Mrs Linde is to be employed by the bank. And I arranged it, Mr Krogstad. Now you know.

KROGSTAD. I guessed right, then.

NORA (*walks up and down the room*). Oh, one has a little influence, you know. Just because one's a woman it doesn't necessarily mean that – When one is in a humble position, Mr Krogstad, one should think twice before offending someone who – hm – !

KROGSTAD. – who has influence?

NORA. Precisely.

KROGSTAD (*changes his tone*). Mrs Helmer, will you have the kindness to use your influence on my behalf?

NORA. What? What do you mean?

KROGSTAD. Will you be so good as to see that I keep my humble position at the bank?

NORA. What do you mean? Who is thinking of removing you from your position?

KROGSTAD. Oh, you don't need to play the innocent with me. I realize it can't be very pleasant for your friend to risk bumping into me. And now I also realize whom I have to thank for being hounded out like this.

NORA. But I assure you –

KROGSTAD. Look, let's not beat about the bush. There's still time, and I'd advise you to use your influence to stop it.

NORA. But, Mr Krogstad, I have no influence!

KROGSTAD. Oh? I thought you just said –

NORA. But I didn't mean it like that! I? How on earth could you imagine that I would have any influence over my husband?

KROGSTAD. Oh, I've known your husband since we were students together. I imagine he has his weaknesses like other married men.

NORA. If you speak impertinently of my husband, I shall show you the door.

KROGSTAD. You're a bold woman, Mrs Helmer.

NORA. I'm not afraid of you any longer. Once the New Year is in, I'll soon be rid of you.

KROGSTAD (*more controlled*). Now listen to me, Mrs Helmer. If I'm forced to, I shall fight for my little job at the bank as I would fight for my life.

NORA. So it sounds.

KROGSTAD. It isn't just the money – that's the last thing I care about. There's something else. Well, you might as well know. It's like this, you see. You know of course, as everyone else does, that some years ago I committed an indiscretion.

NORA. I think I did hear something –

KROGSTAD. It never came into court; but from that day, every opening was barred to me. So I turned my hand to the kind of business you know about. I had to do something; and I don't think I was one of the worst. But now I want to give up all that. My sons are growing up: for their sake, I must try to regain what respectability I can. This job in the bank was the first step on the ladder. And now your husband wants to kick me off that ladder back into the dirt.

NORA. But, my dear Mr Krogstad, it simply isn't in my power to help you.

KROGSTAD. You say that because you don't want to help me. But I have the means to make you.

NORA. You don't mean you'd tell my husband that I owe you money?

KROGSTAD. And if I did?

NORA. That'd be a filthy trick! (*Almost in tears.*) This secret that

is my pride and my joy – that he should hear about it in such a
filthy, beastly way – hear about it from you! It'd involve me in
the most dreadful unpleasantness –

KROGSTAD. Only – unpleasantness?

NORA (*vehemently*). All right, do it! You'll be the one who'll suffer.
It'll show my husband the kind of man you are, and then you'll
never keep your job.

KROGSTAD. I asked you whether it was merely domestic unpleasantness you were afraid of.

NORA. If my husband hears about it, he will of course immediately pay you whatever is owing. And then we shall have nothing
more to do with you.

KROGSTAD (*takes a step closer*). Listen, Mrs Helmer. Either
you've a bad memory or else you know very little about financial
transactions. I had better enlighten you.

NORA. What do you mean?

KROGSTAD. When your husband was ill, you came to me to
borrow two hundred and fifty pounds.

NORA. I didn't know anyone else.

KROGSTAD. I promised to find that sum for you –

NORA. And you did find it.

KROGSTAD. I promised to find that sum for you on certain
conditions. You were so worried about your husband's illness
and so keen to get the money to take him abroad that I don't
think you bothered much about the details. So it won't be out of
place if I refresh your memory. Well – I promised to get you the
money in exchange for an I.O.U., which I drew up.

NORA. Yes, and which I signed.

KROGSTAD. Exactly. But then I added a few lines naming your
father as security for the debt. This paragraph was to be signed
by your father.

NORA. Was to be? He did sign it.

KROGSTAD. I left the date blank for your father to fill in when he
signed this paper. You remember, Mrs Helmer?

NORA. Yes, I think so –

KROGSTAD. Then I gave you back this I.O.U. for you to post to your father. Is that not correct?

NORA. Yes.

KROGSTAD. And of course you posted it at once; for within five or six days you brought it along to me with your father's signature on it. Whereupon I handed you the money.

NORA. Yes, well. Haven't I repaid the instalments as agreed?

KROGSTAD. Mm – yes, more or less. But to return to what we were speaking about – that was a difficult time for you just then, wasn't it, Mrs Helmer?

NORA. Yes, it was.

KROGSTAD. Your father was very ill, if I am not mistaken.

NORA. He was dying.

KROGSTAD. He did in fact die shortly afterwards?

NORA. Yes.

KROGSTAD. Tell me, Mrs Helmer, do you by any chance remember the date of your father's death? The day of the month, I mean.

NORA. Pappa died on the twenty-ninth of September.

KROGSTAD. Quite correct; I took the trouble to confirm it. And that leaves me with a curious little problem – (*Takes out a paper.*) – which I simply cannot solve.

NORA. Problem? I don't see –

KROGSTAD. The problem, Mrs Helmer, is that your father signed this paper three days after his death.

NORA. What? I don't understand –

KROGSTAD. Your father died on the twenty-ninth of September. But look at this. Here your father has dated his signature the second of October. Isn't that a curious little problem, Mrs Helmer?

NORA *is silent.*

KROGSTAD. Can you suggest any explanation?

She remains silent.

KROGSTAD. And there's another curious thing. The words 'second of October' and the year are written in a hand which is not your father's, but which I seem to know. Well, there's a simple explanation to that. Your father could have forgotten to write in the date when he signed, and someone else could have added it before the news came of his death. There's nothing criminal about that. It's the signature itself I'm wondering about. It *is* genuine, I suppose, Mrs Helmer? It was your father who wrote his name here?

NORA (*after a short silence, throws back her head and looks defiantly at him*). No, it was not. It was I who wrote pappa's name there.

KROGSTAD. Look, Mrs Helmer, do you realize this is a dangerous admission?

NORA. Why? You'll get your money.

KROGSTAD. May I ask you a question? Why didn't you send this paper to your father?

NORA. I couldn't. Pappa was very ill. If I'd asked him to sign this, I'd have had to tell him what the money was for. But I couldn't have told him in his condition that my husband's life was in danger. I couldn't have done that!

KROGSTAD. Then you would have been wiser to have given up your idea of a holiday.

NORA. But I couldn't! It was to save my husband's life. I couldn't put it off.

KROGSTAD. But didn't it occur to you that you were being dishonest towards me?

NORA. I couldn't bother about that. I didn't care about you. I hated you because of all the beastly difficulties you'd put in my way when you knew how dangerously ill my husband was.

KROGSTAD. Mrs Helmer, you evidently don't appreciate exactly what you have done. But I can assure you that it is no bigger nor worse a crime than the one I once committed and thereby ruined my whole social position.

NORA. You? Do you expect me to believe that you would have taken a risk like that to save your wife's life?

KROGSTAD. The law does not concern itself with motives.

NORA. Then the law must be very stupid.

KROGSTAD. Stupid or not, if I show this paper to the police, you will be judged according to it.

NORA. I don't believe that. Hasn't a daughter the right to shield her father from worry and anxiety when he's old and dying? Hasn't a wife the right to save her husband's life? I don't know much about the law, but there must be something somewhere that says that such things are allowed. You ought to know that, you're meant to be a lawyer, aren't you? You can't be a very good lawyer, Mr Krogstad.

KROGSTAD. Possibly not. But business, the kind of business we two have been transacting – I think you'll admit I understand something about that? Good. Do as you please. But I tell you this. If I get thrown into the gutter for a second time, I shall take you with me.

He bows and goes out through the hall.

NORA (*stands for a moment in thought, then tosses her head*). What nonsense! He's trying to frighten me! I'm not that stupid. (*Busies herself gathering together the children's clothes; then she suddenly stops.*) But – ? No, it's impossible. I did it for love, didn't I?

CHILDREN (*in the doorway, left*). Mummy, the strange gentleman has gone out into the street.

NORA. Yes, yes, I know. But don't talk to anyone about the strange gentleman. You hear? Not even to Daddy.

CHILDREN. No, Mummy. Will you play with us again now?

NORA. No, no. Not now.

CHILREN. Oh but, Mummy, you promised!

NORA. I know, but I can't just now. Go back to the nursery. I've a lot to do. Go away, my darlings, go away.

She pushes them gently into the other room, and closes the door behind them. She sits on the sofa, takes up her embroidery, stitches for a few moments, but soon stops.

NORA. No! (*Throws the embroidery aside, gets up, goes to the door leading to the hall and calls.*) Helen! Bring in the Christmas tree! (*She goes to the table on the left and opens the drawer in it; then pauses again.*) No, but it's utterly impossible!

MAID (*enters with the tree*). Where shall I put it, madam?

NORA. There, in the middle of the room.

MAID. Will you be wanting anything else?

NORA. No, thank you. I have everything I need.

    The MAID *puts down the tree and goes out.*

NORA (*busy decorating the tree*). Now – candles here – and flowers here. That loathsome man! Nonsense, nonsense, there's nothing to be frightened about. The Christmas tree must be beautiful. I'll do everything that you like, Torvald. I'll sing for you, dance for you –

    HELMER, *with a bundle of papers under his arm, enters.*

NORA. Oh – are you back already?

HELMER. Yes. Has anyone been here?

NORA. Here? No.

HELMER. That's strange. I saw Krogstad come out of the front door.

NORA. Did you? Oh yes, that's quite right – Krogstad was here for a few minutes.

HELMER. Nora, I can tell from your face, he has been here and asked you to put in a good word for him.

NORA. Yes.

HELMER. And you were to pretend you were doing it of your own accord? You weren't going to tell me he'd been here? He asked you to do that too, didn't he?

NORA. Yes, Torvald. But –

HELMER. Nora, Nora! And you were ready to enter into such a conspiracy? Talking to a man like that, and making him promises – and then, on top of it all, to tell me an untruth!

NORA. An untruth?

HELMER. Didn't you say no one had been here? (*Wags his finger.*) My little songbird must never do that again. A songbird must have a clean beak to sing with. Otherwise she'll start twittering out of tune. (*Puts his arm round her waist.*) Isn't that the way we want things? You, of course it is. (*Lets go of her.*) So let's hear no more about that. (*Sits down in front of the stove.*) Ah, how cosy and peaceful it is here! (*Glances for a few moments at his papers.*)

NORA (*busy with the tree; after a short silence*). Torvald.

HELMER. Yes.

NORA. I'm terribly looking forward to that fancy-dress ball at the Stenborgs on Boxing Day.

HELMER. And I'm terribly curious to see what you're going to surprise me with.

NORA. Oh, it's so maddening.

HELMER. What is?

NORA. I can't think of anything to wear. It all seems so stupid and meaningless.

HELMER. So my little Nora has come to that conclusion, has she?

NORA (*behind his chair, resting her arms on its back*). Are you very busy, Torvald?

HELMER. Oh—

NORA. What are those papers?

HELMER. Just something to do with the bank.

NORA. Already?

HELMER. I persuaded the trustees to give me authority to make certain immediate changes in the staff and organization. I want to have everything straight by the New Year.

NORA. Then that's why this poor man Krogstad—

HELMER. Hm.

NORA (*still leaning over his chair, slowly strokes the back of his head*). If you hadn't been so busy, I was going to ask you an enormous favour, Torvald.

HELMER. Well, tell me. What was it to be?

NORA. You know I trust your taste more than anyone's. I'm so anxious to look really beautiful at the fancy-dress ball. Torvald, couldn't you help me to decide what I shall go as, and what kind of costume I ought to wear?

HELMER. Aha! So little Miss Independent's in trouble and needs a man to rescue her, does she?

NORA. Yes, Torvald. I can't get anywhere without your help.

HELMER. Well, well, I'll give the matter thought. We'll find something.

NORA. Oh, how kind of you! (*Goes back to the tree. Pause.*) How pretty these red flowers look! But, tell me, is it so dreadful, this thing that Krogstad's done?

HELMER. He forged someone else's name. Have you any idea what that means?

NORA. Mightn't he have been forced to do it by some emergency?

HELMER. He probably just didn't think – that's what usually happens. I'm not so heartless as to condemn a man for an isolated action.

NORA. No, Torvald, of course not!

HELMER. Men often succeed in re-establishing themselves if they admit their crime and take their punishment.

NORA. Punishment?

HELMER. But Krogstad didn't do that. He chose to try and trick his way out of it. And that's what has morally destroyed him.

NORA. You think that would – ?

HELMER. Just think how a man with that load on his conscience must always be lying and cheating and dissembling – how he must wear a mask even in the presence of those who are dearest to him, even his own wife and children! Yes, the children. That's the worst danger, Nora.

NORA. Why?

HELMER. Because an atmosphere of lies contaminates and poisons every corner of the home. Every breath that the children draw in such a house contains the germs of evil.

NORA (*comes closer behind him*). Do you really believe that?

HELMER. Oh, my dear, I've come across it so often in my work at the bar. Nearly all young criminals are the children of mothers who are constitutional liars.

NORA. Why do you say mothers?

HELMER. It's usually the mother – though of course the father can have the same influence. Every lawyer knows that only too well. And yet this fellow Krogstad has been sitting at home all these years poisoning his children with his lies and pretences. That's why I say that, morally speaking, he is dead. (*Stretches out his hand towards her.*) So my pretty little Nora must promise me not to plead his case. Your hand on it. Come, come, what's this? Give me your hand. There. That's settled, now. I assure you it'd be quite impossible for me to work in the same building as him. I literally feel physically ill in the presence of a man like that.

NORA (*draws her hand from his and goes over to the other side of the Christmas tree*). How hot it is in here! And I've so much to do.

HELMER (*gets up and gathers his papers*). Yes, and I must try to get some of this read before dinner. I'll think about your costume too. And I may even have something up my sleeve to hang in gold paper on the Christmas tree. (*Lays his hand on her head.*) My precious little songbird!

He goes into his study and closes the door.

NORA (*softly, after a pause*). It's nonsense. It must be. It's impossible. It *must* be impossible!

NURSE (*in the doorway, left*). The children are asking if they can come in to Mummy.

NORA. No, no, no – don't let them in. You stay with them, Anne-Marie.

NURSE. Very good, madam. (*Closes the door.*)

NORA (*pale with fear*). Corrupt my little children – ! Poison my home! (*Short pause. She throws back her head.*) It isn't true! It *couldn't* be true!

ACT TWO

The same room. In the corner by the piano the Christmas tree stands, stripped and dishevelled, its candles burned to their sockets. NORA's *outdoor clothes lie on the sofa. She is alone in the room, walking restlessly to and fro. At length she stops by the sofa and picks up her coat.*

NORA (*drops the coat again*). There's someone coming! (*Goes to the door and listens.*) No, it's no one. Of course – no one'll come today, it's Christmas Day. Nor tomorrow. But perhaps – ! (*Opens the door and looks out.*) No. Nothing in the letter-box. Quite empty. (*Walks across the room.*) Silly, silly. Of course he won't do anything. It couldn't happen. It isn't possible. Why, I've three small children.

The NURSE, *carrying a large cardboard box, enters from the room on the left.*

NURSE. I found those fancy dress clothes at last, madam.

NORA. Thank you. Put them on the table.

NURSE (*does so*). They're all rumpled up.

NORA. Oh, I wish I could tear them into a million pieces!

NURSE. Why, madam! They'll be all right. Just a little patience.

NORA. Yes, of course. I'll go and get Mrs Linde to help me.

NURSE. What, out again? In this dreadful weather? You'll catch a chill, madam.

NORA. Well, that wouldn't be the worst. How are the children?

NURSE. Playing with their Christmas presents, poor little dears. But –

NORA. Are they still asking to see me?

NURSE. They're so used to having their mummy with them.

NORA. Yes, but, Anne-Marie, from now on I shan't be able to spend so much time with them.

NURSE. Well, children get used to anything in time.

NORA. Do you think so? Do you think they'd forget their mother if she went away from them – for ever?

NURSE. Mercy's sake, madam! For ever!

NORA. Tell me, Anne-Marie – I've so often wondered. How could you bear to give your child away – to strangers?

NURSE. But I had to when I came to nurse my little Miss Nora.

NORA. Do you mean you wanted to?

NURSE. When I had the chance of such a good job? A poor girl what's got into trouble can't afford to pick and choose. That good-for-nothing didn't lift a finger.

NORA. But your daughter must have completely forgotten you.

NURSE. Oh no, indeed she hasn't. She's written to me twice, once when she got confirmed and then again when she got married.

NORA (*hugs her*). Dear old Anne-Marie, you were a good mother to me.

NURSE. Poor little Miss Nora, you never had any mother but me.

NORA. And if my little ones had no one else, I know you would – no, silly, silly, silly! (*Opens the cardboard box.*) Go back to them, Anne-Marie. Now I must – ! Tomorrow you'll see how pretty I shall look.

NURSE. Why, there'll be no one at the ball as beautiful as my Miss Nora.

She goes into the room, left.

NORA (*begins to unpack the clothes from the box, but soon throws them down again*). Oh, if only I dared go out! If I could be sure no one would come and nothing would happen while I was away! Stupid, stupid! No one will come. I just mustn't think about it. Brush this muff. Pretty gloves, pretty gloves! Don't think about it, don't think about it! One, two, three, four, five, six – (*Cries.*) Ah – they're coming – !

She begins to run towards the door, but stops uncertainly. MRS LINDE *enters from the hall, where she has been taking off her outdoor clothes.*

NORA. Oh, it's you, Christine. There's no one else outside, is there? Oh, I'm so glad you've come.

MRS LINDE. I hear you were at my room asking for me.

NORA. Yes, I just happened to be passing. I want to ask you to help me with something. Let's sit down here on the sofa. Look at this. There's going to be a fancy-dress ball tomorrow night upstairs at Consul Stenborg's, and Torvald wants me to go as a Neapolitan fisher-girl and dance the tarantella. I learned it in Capri.

MRS LINDE. I say, are you going to give a performance?

NORA. Yes, Torvald says I should. Look, here's the dress. Torvald had it made for me in Italy – but now it's all so torn, I don't know –

MRS LINDE. Oh, we'll soon put that right – the stitching's just come away. Needle and thread? Ah, here we are.

NORA. You're being awfully sweet.

MRS LINDE (*sews*). So you're going to dress up tomorrow, Nora? I must pop over for a moment to see how you look. Oh, but I've completely forgotten to thank you for that nice evening yesterday.

NORA (*gets up and walks across the room*). Oh, I didn't think it was as nice as usual. You ought to have come to town a little earlier, Christine. . . . Yes, Torvald understands how to make a home look attractive.

MRS LINDE. I'm sure you do, too. You're not your father's daughter for nothing. But, tell me – is Dr Rank always in such low spirits as he was yesterday?

NORA. No, last night it was very noticeable. But he's got a terrible disease – he's got spinal tuberculosis, poor man. His father was a frightful creature who kept mistresses and so on. As a result Dr Rank has been sickly ever since he was a child – you understand –

MRS LINDE (*puts down her sewing*). But, my dear Nora, how on earth did you get to know about such things?

NORA (*walks about the room*). Oh, don't be silly, Christine – when one has three children, one comes into contact with women who – well, who know about medical matters, and they tell one a thing or two.

MRS LINDE (*sews again; a short silence*). Does Dr Rank visit you every day?

NORA. Yes, every day. He's Torvald's oldest friend, and a good friend to me too. Dr Rank's almost one of the family.

MRS LINDE. But, tell me – is he quite sincere? I mean, doesn't he rather say the sort of thing he thinks people want to hear?

NORA. No, quite the contrary. What gave you that idea?

MRS LINDE. When you introduced me to him yesterday, he said he'd often heard my name mentioned here. But later I noticed your husband had no idea who I was. So how could Dr Rank –

NORA. Yes, that's quite right, Christine. You see, Torvald's so hopelessly in love with me that he wants to have me all to himself – those were his very words. When we were first married, he got quite jealous if I as much as mentioned any of my old friends back home. So naturally, I stopped talking about them. But I often chat with Dr Rank about that kind of thing. He enjoys it, you see.

MRS LINDE. Now listen, Nora. In many ways you're still a child; I'm a bit older than you and have a little more experience of the world. There's something I want to say to you. You ought to give up this business with Dr Rank.

NORA. What business?

MRS LINDE. Well, everything. Last night you were speaking about this rich admirer of yours who was going to give you money –

NORA. Yes, and who doesn't exist – unfortunately. But what's that got to do with – ?

MRS LINDE. Is Dr Rank rich?

NORA. Yes.

MRS LINDE. And he has no dependants?

NORA. No, no one. But –

MRS LINDE. And he comes here to see you every day?

NORA. Yes, I've told you.

MRS LINDE. But how dare a man of his education be so forward?

NORA. What on earth are you talking about?

MRS LINDE. Oh, stop pretending, Nora. Do you think I haven't guessed who it was who lent you that two hundred pounds?

NORA. Are you out of your mind? How could you imagine such a thing? A friend, someone who comes here every day! Why, that'd be an impossible situation!

MRS LINDE. Then it really wasn't him?

NORA. No, of course not. I've never for a moment dreamed of – anyway, he hadn't any money to lend then. He didn't come into that till later.

MRS LINDE. Well, I think that was a lucky thing for you, Nora dear.

NORA. No, I could never have dreamed of asking Dr Rank – Though I'm sure that if ever I did ask him –

MRS LINDE. But of course you won't.

NORA. Of course not. I can't imagine that it should ever become necessary. But I'm perfectly sure that if I did speak to Dr Rank –

MRS LINDE. Behind your husband's back?

NORA. I've got to get out of this other business – and *that's* been going on behind his back. I've *got* to get out of it.

MRS LINDE. Yes, well, that's what I told you yesterday. But –

NORA (*walking up and down*). It's much easier for a man to arrange these things than a woman –

MRS LINDE. One's own husband, yes.

NORA. Oh, bosh. (*Stops walking.*) When you've completely repaid a debt, you get your I.O.U. back, don't you?

MRS LINDE. Yes, of course.

NORA. And you can tear it into a thousand pieces and burn the filthy, beastly thing!

MRS LINDE (*looks hard at her, puts down her sewing and gets up slowly*). Nora, you're hiding something from me.

NORA. Can you see that?

MRS LINDE. Something has happened since yesterday morning. Nora, what is it?

NORA (*goes towards her*). Christine! (*Listens.*) Ssh! There's Torvald. Would you mind going into the nursery for a few minutes? Torvald can't bear to see sewing around. Anne-Marie'll help you.

MRS LINDE (*gathers some of her things together*). Very well. But I shan't leave this house until we've talked this matter out.

She goes into the nursery, left. As she does so, HELMER *enters from the hall.*

NORA (*runs to meet him*). Oh, Torvald dear, I've been so longing for you to come back!

HELMER. Was that the dressmaker?

NORA. No, it was Christine. She's helping me mend my costume. I'm going to look rather splendid in that.

HELMER. Yes, that was quite a bright idea of mine, wasn't it?

NORA. Wonderful! But wasn't it nice of me to give in to you?

HELMER (*takes her chin in his hand*). Nice - to give in to your husband? All right, little silly, I know you didn't mean it like that. But I won't disturb you. I expect you'll be wanting to try it on.

NORA. Are you going to work now?

HELMER. Yes. (*Shows her a bundle of papers.*) Look at these. I've been down to the bank - (*Turns to go into his study.*)

NORA. Torvald.

HELMER (*stops*). Yes.

NORA. If little squirrel asked you really prettily to grant her a wish -

HELMER. Well?

NORA. Would you grant it to her?

HELMER. First I should naturally have to know what it was.

NORA. Squirrel would do lots of pretty tricks for you if you granted her wish.

HELMER. Out with it, then.

NORA. Your little skylark would sing in every room –

HELMER. My little skylark does that already.

NORA. I'd turn myself into a little fairy and dance for you in the moonlight, Torvald.

HELMER. Nora, it isn't that business you were talking about this morning?

NORA (*comes closer*). Yes, Torvald – oh, please! I beg of you!

HELMER. Have you really the nerve to bring that up again?

NORA. Yes, Torvald, yes, you must do as I ask! You must let Krogstad keep his place at the bank!

HELMER. My dear Nora, his is the job I'm giving to Mrs Linde.

NORA. Yes, that's terribly sweet of you. But you can get rid of one of the other clerks instead of Krogstad.

HELMER. Really, you're being incredibly obstinate. Just because you thoughtlessly promised to put in a word for him, you expect me to –

NORA. No, it isn't that, Helmer. It's for your own sake. That man writes for the most beastly newspapers – you said so yourself. He could do you tremendous harm. I'm so dreadfully frightened of him –

HELMER. Oh, I understand. Memories of the past. That's what's frightening you.

NORA. What do you mean?

HELMER. You're thinking of your father, aren't you?

NORA. Yes, yes. Of course. Just think what those dreadful men wrote in the papers about papa! The most frightful slanders. I really believe it would have lost him his job if the Ministry hadn't sent you down to investigate, and you hadn't been so kind and helpful to him.

HELMER. But, my dear little Nora, there's a considerable difference between your father and me. Your father was not a man of unassailable reputation. But I am. And I hope to remain so all my life.

NORA. But no one knows what spiteful people may not dig up. We could be so peaceful and happy now, Torvald – we could be free from every worry – you and I and the children. Oh, please, Torvald, please – !

HELMER. The very fact of your pleading his cause makes it impossible for me to keep him. Everyone at the bank already knows that I intend to dismiss Krogstad. If the rumour got about that the new vice-president had allowed his wife to persuade him to change his mind –

NORA. Well, what then?

HELMER. Oh, nothing, nothing. As long as my little Miss Obstinate gets her way – ! Do you expect me to make a laughingstock of myself before my entire staff – give people the idea that I am open to outside influence? Believe me, I'd soon feel the consequences! Besides – there's something else that makes it impossible for Krogstad to remain in the bank while I am its manager.

NORA. What is that?

HELMER. I might conceivably have allowed myself to ignore his moral obloquies –

NORA. Yes, Torvald, surely?

HELMER. And I hear he's quite efficient at his job. But we – well, we were school friends. It was one of those friendships that one enters into over-hastily and so often comes to regret later in life. I might as well confess the truth. We – well, we're on Christian name terms. And the tactless idiot makes no attempt to conceal it when other people are present. On the contrary, he thinks it gives him the right to be familiar with me. He shows off the whole time, with 'Torvald this', and 'Torvald that'. I can tell you, I find it damned annoying. If he stayed, he'd make my position intolerable.

NORA. Torvald, you can't mean this seriously.

HELMER. Oh? And why not?

NORA. But it's so petty.

HELMER. What did you say? Petty? You think I am petty?

NORA. No, Torvald dear, of course you're not. That's just why –

HELMER. Don't quibble! You call my motives petty. Then I

must be petty too. Petty! I see. Well, I've had enough of this. (*Goes to the door and calls into the hall.*) Helen!

NORA. What are you going to do?

HELMER (*searching among his papers*). I'm going to settle this matter once and for all.

The MAID *enters.*

HELMER. Take this letter downstairs at once. Find a messenger and see that he delivers it. Immediately! The address is on the envelope. Here's the money.

MAID. Very good, sir. (*Goes out with the letter.*)

HELMER (*putting his papers in order*). There now, little Miss Obstinate.

NORA (*tensely*). Torvald – what was in that letter?

HELMER. Krogstad's dismissal.

NORA. Call her back, Torvald! There's still time. Oh, Torvald, call her back! Do it for my sake – for your own sake – for the children! Do you hear me, Torvald? Please do it! You don't realize what this may do to us all!

HELMER. Too late.

NORA. Yes. Too late.

HELMER. My dear Nora, I forgive you this anxiety. Though it is a bit of an insult to me. Oh, but it is! Isn't it an insult to imply that I should be frightened by the vindictiveness of a depraved hack journalist? But I forgive you, because it so charmingly testifies to the love you bear me. (*Takes her in his arms.*) Which is as it should be, my own dearest Nora. Let what will happen, happen. When the real crisis comes, you will not find me lacking in strength or courage. I am man enough to bear the burden for us both.

NORA (*fearfully*). What do you mean?

HELMER. The whole burden, I say –

NORA (*calmly*). I shall never let you do that.

HELMER. Very well. We shall share it, Nora – as man and wife. And that's as it should be. (*Caresses her.*) Are you happy now? There, there, there; don't look at me with those frightened little eyes. You're simply imagining things. You go ahead now and do your tarantella, and get some practice on that tambourine. I'll sit in my study and close the door. Then I won't hear anything, and you can make all the noise you want. (*Turns in the doorway.*) When Dr Rank comes, tell him where to find me. (*He nods to her, goes into his room with his papers and closes the door.*)

NORA (*desperate with anxiety, stands as though transfixed, and whispers*). He said he'd do it. He will do it. He will do it, and nothing'll stop him. No, never that. I'd rather anything. There must be some escape – Some way out – !

The bell rings in the hall.

NORA. Dr Rank – ! Anything but that! Anything, I don't care – !
She passes her hand across her face, composes herself, walks across and opens the door to the hall. DR RANK *is standing there, hanging up his fur coat. During the following scene it begins to grow dark.*

NORA. Good evening, Dr Rank. I recognized your ring. But you mustn't go in to Torvald yet. I think he's busy.

RANK. And – you?

NORA (*as he enters the room and she closes the door behind him*). Oh, you know very well I've always time to talk to you.

RANK. Thank you. I shall avail myself of that privilege as long as I can.

NORA. What do you mean by that? As long as you *can*?

RANK. Yes. Does that frighten you?

NORA. Well, it's rather a curious expression. Is something going to happen?

RANK. Something I've been expecting to happen for a long time. But I didn't think it would happen quite so soon.

NORA (*seizes his arm*). What is it? Dr Rank, you must tell me!

RANK (*sits down by the stove*). I'm on the way out. And there's nothing to be done about it.

NORA (*sighs with relief*). Oh, it's you – ?

RANK. Who else? No, it's no good lying to oneself. I am the

most wretched of all my patients, Mrs Helmer. These last few days I've been going through the books of this poor body of mine, and I find I am bankrupt. Within a month I may be rotting up there in the churchyard.

NORA. Ugh, what a nasty way to talk!

RANK. The facts aren't exactly nice. But the worst is that there's so much else that's nasty that's got to come first. I've only one more test to make. When that's done I'll have a pretty accurate idea of when the final disintegration is likely to begin. I want to ask you a favour. Helmer's a sensitive chap, and I know how he hates anything ugly. I don't want him to visit me when I'm in hospital –

NORA. Oh but, Dr Rank –

RANK. I don't want him there. On any pretext. I shan't have him allowed in. As soon as I know the worst, I'll send you my visiting card with a black cross on it, and then you'll know that the final filthy process has begun.

NORA. Really, you're being quite impossible this evening. And I did hope you'd be in a good mood.

RANK. With death on my hands? And all this to atone for someone else's sin? Is there justice in that? And in every single family, in one way or another, the same merciless law of retribution is at work –

NORA (holds her hands to her ears). Nonsense! Cheer up! Laugh!

RANK. Yes, you're right. Laughter's all the damned thing's fit for. My poor innocent spine must pay for the fun my father had as a gay young lieutenant.

NORA (at the table, left). You mean he was too fond of asparagus and foie gras?

RANK. Yes; and truffles too.

NORA. Yes, of course, truffles, yes. And oysters too, I suppose?

RANK. Yes, oysters, oysters. Of course.

NORA. And all that port and champagne to wash them down. It's too sad that all those lovely things should affect one's spine.

RANK. Especially a poor spine that never got any pleasure out of them.

NORA. Oh yes, that's the saddest thing of all.

RANK (*looks searchingly at her*). Hm –

NORA (*after a moment*). Why did you smile?

RANK. No, it was you who laughed.

NORA. No, it was you who smiled, Dr Rank!

RANK (*gets up*). You're a worse little rogue than I thought.

NORA. Oh, I'm full of stupid tricks today.

RANK. So it seems.

NORA. (*puts both her hands on his shoulders*). Dear, dear Dr Rank, you mustn't die and leave Torvald and me.

RANK. Oh, you'll soon get over it. Once one is gone, one is soon forgotten.

NORA (*looks at him anxiously*). Do you believe that?

RANK. One finds replacements, and then –

NORA. Who will find a replacement?

RANK. You and Helmer both will, when I am gone. You seem to have made a start already, haven't you? What was this Mrs Linde doing here yesterday evening?

NORA. Aha! But surely you can't be jealous of poor Christine?

RANK. Indeed I am. She will be my successor in this house. When I have moved on, this lady will –

NORA. Ssh – don't speak so loud! She's in there!

RANK. Today again? You see!

NORA. She's only come to mend my dress. Good heavens, how unreasonable you are! (*Sits on the sofa.*) Be nice now, Dr Rank. Tomorrow you'll see how beautifully I shall dance; and you must imagine I'm doing it just for you. And for Torvald, of course – obviously. (*Takes some things out of the box.*) Dr Rank, sit down here and I'll show you something.

RANK (*sits*). What's this?

NORA. Look here! Look!

RANK. Silk stockings!

NORA. Flesh-coloured. Aren't they beautiful? It's very dark in here now, of course, but tomorrow – ! No, no, no – only the soles. Oh well, I suppose you can look a bit higher if you want to.

RANK. Hm –

NORA. Why are you looking so critical? Don't you think they'll fit me?

RANK. I can't really give you a qualified opinion on that.

NORA (*looks at him for a moment*). Shame on you! (*Flicks him on the ear with the stockings.*) Take that. (*Puts them back in the box.*)

RANK. What other wonders are to be revealed to me?

NORA. I shan't show you anything else. You're being naughty.

She hums a little and looks among the things in the box.

RANK (*after a short silence*). When I sit here like this being so intimate with you, I can't think – I cannot imagine what would have become of me if I had never entered this house.

NORA (*smiles*). Yes, I think you enjoy being with us, don't you?

RANK (*more quietly, looking into the middle distance*). And now to have to leave it all –

NORA. Nonsense. You're not leaving us.

RANK (*as before*). And not to be able to leave even the most wretched token of gratitude behind; hardly even a passing sense of loss; only an empty space, to be filled by the next comer.

NORA. Suppose I were to ask you to – ? No –

RANK. To do what?

NORA. To give me proof of your friendship –

RANK. Yes, yes?

NORA. No, I mean – to do me a very great service –

RANK. Would you really for once grant me that happiness?

NORA. But you've no idea what it is.

RANK. Very well, tell me, then.

NORA. No, but, Dr Rank, I can't. It's far too much – I want your help and advice, and I want you to do something for me.

RANK. The more the better. I've no idea what it can be. But tell me. You do trust me, don't you?

NORA. Oh, yes, more than anyone. You're my best and truest friend. Otherwise I couldn't tell you. Well then, Dr Rank, there's something you must help me to prevent. You know how much Torvald loves me - he'd never hesitate for an instant to lay down his life for me -

RANK (*leans over towards her*). Nora - do you think he is the only one - ?

NORA (*with a slight start*). What do you mean?

RANK. Who would gladly lay down his life for you?

NORA (*sadly*). Oh, I see.

RANK. I swore to myself I would let you know that before I go. I shall never have a better opportunity. . . . Well, Nora, now you know that. And now you also know that you can trust me as you can trust nobody else.

NORA (*rises; calmly and quietly*). Let me pass, please

RANK (*makes room for her but remains seated*). Nora -

NORA (*in the doorway to the hall*). Helen, bring the lamp. (*Goes over to the stove.*) Oh, dear, Dr Rank, this was really horrid of you.

RANK (*gets up*). That I have loved you as deeply as anyone else has? Was that horrid of me?

NORA. No - but that you should go and tell me. That was quite unnecessary -

RANK. What do you mean? Did you know, then - ?

The MAID *enters with the lamp, puts it on the table and goes out.*

RANK. Nora - Mrs Helmer! I am asking you, did you know this?

NORA. Oh, what do I know, what did I know, what didn't I know - ? I really can't say. How could you be so stupid, Dr Rank? Everything was so nice.

RANK. Well, at any rate, now you know that I am ready to serve you, body and soul. So - please continue.

NORA (*looks at him*). After this?

RANK. Please tell me what it is.

NORA. I can't possibly tell you now.

RANK. Yes, yes! You mustn't punish me like this. Let me be allowed to do what I can for you.

NORA. You can't do anything for me now. Anyway, I don't need any help. It was only my imagination – you'll see. Yes, really. Honestly. (*Sits in the rocking-chair, looks at him and smiles.*) Well, upon my word you *are* a fine gentleman, Dr Rank. Aren't you ashamed of yourself, now that the lamp's been lit?

RANK. Frankly, no. But perhaps I ought to say – *adieu?*

NORA. Of course not. You will naturally continue to visit us as before. You know quite well how Torvald depends on your company.

RANK. Yes, but you?

NORA. Oh, I always think it's enormous fun having you here.

RANK. That was what misled me. You're a riddle to me, you know. I'd often felt you'd just as soon be with me as with Helmer.

NORA. Well, you see, there are some people whom one loves, and others whom it's almost more fun to be with.

RANK. Oh, yes, there's some truth in that.

NORA. When I was at home, of course, I loved papa best. But I always used to think it was terribly amusing to go down and talk to the servants; because they never told me what I ought to do; and they were such fun to listen to.

RANK. I see. So I've taken their place?

NORA (*jumps up and runs over to him*). Oh, dear, sweet Dr Rank, I didn't mean that at all. But I'm sure you understand – I feel the same about Torvald as I did about papa.

MAID (*enters from the hall*). Excuse me, madam. (*Whispers to her and hands her a visiting card.*)

NORA (*glances at the card*). Oh! (*Puts it quickly in her pocket.*)

RANK. Anything wrong?

NORA. No, no, nothing at all. It's just something that – it's my new dress.

RANK. What? But your costume is lying over there.

NORA. Oh – that, yes – but there's another – I ordered it specially
– Torvald mustn't know –

RANK. Ah, so that's your big secret?

NORA. Yes, yes. Go in and talk to him – he's in his study – keep
him talking for a bit –

RANK. Don't worry. He won't get away from me. (*Goes into*
HELMER's *study*.)

NORA (*to the* MAID). Is he waiting in the kitchen?

MAID. Yes, madam, he came up the back way –

NORA. But didn't you tell him I had a visitor?

MAID. Yes, but he wouldn't go.

NORA. Wouldn't go?

MAID. No, madam, not until he's spoken with you.

NORA. Very well, show him in. But quietly. Helen, you mustn't
tell anyone about this. It's a surprise for my husband.

MAID. Very good, madam. I understand. (*Goes*.)

NORA. It's happening. It's happening after all. No, no, no, it
can't happen, it mustn't happen.

> She walks across and bolts the door of HELMER's study. The
> MAID opens the door from the hall to admit KROGSTAD, and
> closes it behind him. He is wearing an overcoat, heavy boots and
> a fur cap.

NORA (*goes towards him*). Speak quietly. My husband's at home.

KROGSTAD. Let him hear.

NORA. What do you want from me?

KROGSTAD. Information.

NORA. Hurry up, then. What is it?

KROGSTAD. I suppose you know I've been given the sack.

NORA. I couldn't stop it, Mr Krogstad. I did my best for you, but
it didn't help.

KROGSTAD. Does your husband love you so little? He knows
what I can do to you, and yet he dares to –

NORA. Surely you don't imagine I told him?

KROGSTAD. No, I didn't really think you had. It wouldn't have

been like my old friend Torvald Helmer to show that much
courage –

NORA. Mr Krogstad, I'll trouble you to speak respectfully of
my husband.

KROGSTAD. Don't worry, I'll show him all the respect he
deserves. But since you're so anxious to keep this matter
hushed up, I presume you're better informed than you were
yesterday of the gravity of what you've done?

NORA. I've learned more than you could ever teach me.

KROGSTAD. Yes, a bad lawyer like me –

NORA. What do you want from me?

KROGSTAD. I just wanted to see how things were with you, Mrs
Helmer. I've been thinking about you all day. Even duns and
hack journalists have hearts, you know.

NORA. Show some heart, then. Think of my little children.

KROGSTAD. Have you and your husband thought of mine? Well,
let's forget that. I just wanted to tell you, you don't need to take
this business too seriously. I'm not going to take any action, for
the present.

NORA. Oh, no – you won't will you? I knew it.

KROGSTAD. It can all be settled quite amicably. There's no need
for it to become public. We'll keep it among the three of us.

NORA. My husband must never know about this.

KROGSTAD. How can you stop him? Can you pay the balance of
what you owe me?

NORA. Not immediately.

KROGSTAD. Have you any means of raising the money during the
next few days?

NORA. None that I would care to use.

KROGSTAD. Well, it wouldn't have helped anyway. However
much money you offered me now I wouldn't give you back
that paper.

NORA. What are you going to do with it?

KROGSTAD. Just keep it. No one else need ever hear about it.
So in case you were thinking of doing anything desperate –

NORA. I am.

KROGSTAD. Such as running away –

NORA. I am.

KROGSTAD. Or anything more desperate –

NORA. How did you know?

KROGSTAD. – just give up the idea.

NORA. How did you know?

KROGSTAD. Most of us think of that at first. I did. But I hadn't the courage –

NORA (*dully*). Neither have I.

KROGSTAD (*relieved*). It's true, isn't it? You haven't the courage, either?

NORA. No. I haven't. I haven't.

KROGSTAD. It'd be a stupid thing to do anyway. Once the first little domestic explosion is over ... I've got a letter in my pocket here addressed to your husband –

NORA. Telling him everything?

KROGSTAD. As delicately as possible.

NORA (*quickly*). He must never see that letter. Tear it up. I'll find the money somehow –

KROGSTAD. I'm sorry, Mrs Helmer, I thought I'd explained –

NORA. Oh, I don't mean the money I owe you. Let me know how much you want from my husband, and I'll find it for you.

KROGSTAD. I'm not asking your husband for money.

NORA. What do you want, then?

KROGSTAD. I'll tell you. I want to get on my feet again, Mrs Helmer. I want to get to the top. And your husband's going to help me. For eighteen months now my record's been clean. I've been in hard straits all that time: I was content to fight my way back inch by inch. Now I've been chucked back into the mud, and I'm not going to be satisfied with just getting back my job. I'm going to get to the top, I tell you. I'm going to get back into the bank, and it's going to be higher up. Your husband's going to create a new job for me –

NORA. He'll never do that!

KROGSTAD. Oh yes, he will. I know him. He won't dare to risk a scandal. And once I'm in there with him, you'll see! Within a year I'll be his right-hand man. It'll be Nils Krogstad who'll be running that bank, not Torvald Helmer!

NORA. That will never happen.

KROGSTAD. Are you thinking of – ?

NORA. Now I *have* the courage.

KROGSTAD. Oh, you can't frighten me. A pampered little pretty like you –

NORA. You'll see! You'll see!

KROGSTAD. Under the ice? Down in the cold, black water? And then, in the spring, to float up again, ugly, unrecognizable, hairless – ?

NORA. You can't frighten me.

KROGSTAD. And you can't frighten me. People don't do such things, Mrs Helmer. And anyway, what'd be the use? I've got him in my pocket.

NORA. But afterwards? When I'm no longer – ?

KROGSTAD. Have you forgotten that then your reputation will be in my hands?

She looks at him speechlessly.

KROGSTAD. Well, I've warned you. Don't do anything silly. When Helmer's read my letter, he'll get in touch with me. And remember, it's your husband who has forced me to act like this. And for that I'll never forgive him. Goodbye, Mrs Helmer. (*He goes out through the hall.*)

NORA (*runs to the hall door, opens it a few inches and listens*). He's going. He's not going to give him the letter. Oh, no, no, it couldn't possibly happen. (*Opens the door, a little wider.*) What's he doing? Standing outside the front door. He's not going downstairs. Is he changing his mind? Yes, he – !

A letter falls into the letter-box. KROGSTAD's *footsteps die away down the stairs.*

NORA (*with a stifled cry, runs across the room towards the table by the sofa. A pause*). In the letter-box. (*Steals timidly over towards the hall door.*) There it is! Oh, Torvald, Torvald! Now we're lost!

MRS LINDE (*enters from the nursery with* NORA'*s costume*). Well, I've done the best I can. Shall we see how it looks – ?

NORA (*whispers hoarsely*). Christine, come here.

MRS LINDE (*throws the dress on the sofa*). What's wrong with you? You look as though you'd seen a ghost!

NORA. Come here. Do you see that letter? There – look – through the glass of the letter-box.

MRS LINDE. Yes, yes, I see it.

NORA. That letter's from Krogstad –

MRS LINDE. Nora! It was Krogstad who lent you the money!

NORA. Yes. And now Torvald's going to discover everything.

MRS LINDE. Oh, believe me, Nora, it'll be best for you both.

NORA. You don't know what's happened. I've committed a forgery –

MRS LINDE. But, for heaven's sake – !

NORA. Christine, all I want is for you to be my witness.

MRS LINDE. What do you mean? Witness what?

NORA. If I should go out of my mind – and it might easily happen –

MRS LINDE. Nora!

NORA. Or if anything else should happen to me – so that I wasn't here any longer –

MRS LINDE. Nora, Nora, you don't know what you're saying!

NORA. If anyone should try to take the blame, and say it was all his fault – you understand – ?

MRS LINDE. Yes, yes – but how can you think – ?

NORA. Then you must testify that it isn't true, Christine. I'm not mad – I know exactly what I'm saying – and I'm telling you, no one else knows anything about this. I did it entirely on my own. Remember that.

MRS LINDE. All right. But I simply don't understand –

NORA. Oh, how could you understand? A – miracle – is about to happen.

MRS LINDE. Miracle?

NORA. Yes. A miracle. But it's so frightening, Christine. It mustn't happen, not for anything in the world.

MRS LINDE. I'll go over and talk to Krogstad.

NORA. Don't go near him. He'll only do something to hurt you.

MRS LINDE. Once upon a time he'd have done anything for my sake.

NORA. He?

MRS LINDE. Where does he live?

NORA. Oh, how should I know – ? Oh yes, wait a moment – ! (*Feels in her pocket.*) Here's his card. But the letter, the letter – !

HELMER(*from his study, knocks on the door*). Nora!

NORA (*cries in alarm*). What is it?

HELMER. Now, now, don't get alarmed. We're not coming in – you've closed the door. Are you trying on your costume?

NORA. Yes, yes – I'm trying on my costume. I'm going to look so pretty for you, Torvald.

MRS LINDE (*who has been reading the card*). Why, he lives just round the corner.

NORA. Yes; but it's no use. There's nothing to be done now. The letter's lying there in the box.

MRS LINDE. And your husband has the key?

NORA. Yes, he always keeps it.

MRS LINDE. Krogstad must ask him to send the letter back unread. He must find some excuse –

NORA. But Torvald always opens the box at just about this time –

MRS LINDE. You must stop him. Go in and keep him talking. I'll be back as quickly as I can.

She hurries out through the hall.

NORA (*goes over to* HELMER's *door, opens it and peeps in*). Torvald!

HELMER (*offstage*). Well, may a man enter his own drawing-room again? Come on, Rank, now we'll see what – (*In the doorway.*) But what's this?

NORA. What, Torvald dear?

HELMER. Rank's been preparing me for some great transformation scene.

RANK (*in the doorway*). So I understood. But I seem to have been mistaken.

NORA. Yes, no one's to be allowed to see me before tomorrow night.

HELMER. But, my dear Nora, you look quite worn out. Have you been practising too hard?

NORA. No, I haven't practised at all yet.

HELMER. Well, you must.

NORA. Yes, Torvald, I must, I know. But I can't get anywhere without your help. I've completely forgotten everything.

HELMER. Oh, we'll soon put that to rights.

NORA. Yes, help me, Torvald. Promise me you will? Oh, I'm so nervous. All those people – ! You must forget everything except me this evening. You mustn't think of business – I won't even let you touch a pen. Promise me, Torvald?

HELMER. I promise. This evening I shall think of nothing but you – my poor, helpless little darling. Oh, there's just one thing I must see to – (*Goes towards the hall door.*)

NORA. What do you want out there?

HELMER. I'm only going to see if any letters have come.

NORA. No, Torvald, no!

HELMER. Why what's the matter?

NORA. Torvald, I beg you. There's nothing there.

HELMER. Well, I'll just make sure.

> *He moves towards the door.* NORA *runs to the piano and plays the first bars of the* Tarantella.

HELMER (*at the door, turns*). Aha!

NORA. I can't dance tomorrow if I don't practise with you now.

HELMER (*goes over to her*). Are you really so frightened, Nora dear?

NORA. Yes, terribly frightened. Let me start practising now, at once – we've still time before dinner. Oh, do sit down and play for me, Torvald dear. Correct me, lead me, the way you always do.

HELMER. Very well, my dear, if you wish it.

He sits down at the piano. NORA *seizes the tambourine and a long multi-coloured shawl from the cardboard box, wraps the shawl hastily around her, then takes a quick leap into the centre of the room and cries.*

NORA. Play for me! I want to dance!

HELMER *plays and* NORA *dances.* DR RANK *stands behind* HELMER *at the piano and watches her.*

HELMER (*as he plays*). Slower, slower!

NORA. I can't!

HELMER. Not so violently, Nora.

NORA. I must!

HELMER (*stops playing*). No, no, this won't do at all.

NORA (*laughs and swings her tambourine*). Isn't that what I told you?

RANK. Let me play for her.

HELMER (*gets up*). Yes, would you? Then it'll be easier for me to show her.

RANK *sits down at the piano and plays.* NORA *dances more and more wildly.* HELMER *has stationed himself by the stove and tries repeatedly to correct her, but she seems not to hear him. Her hair works loose and falls over her shoulders; she ignores it and continues to dance.* MRS LINDE *enters.*

MRS LINDE (*stands in the doorway as though tongue-tied*). Ah – !

NORA (*as she dances*). Oh, Christine, we're having such fun!

HELMER. But, Nora darling, you're dancing as if your life depended on it.

NORA. It does.

HELMER. Rank, stop it! This is sheer lunacy. Stop it, I say!

RANK *ceases playing.* NORA *suddenly stops dancing.*

HELMER (*goes over to her*). I'd never have believed it. You've forgotten everything I taught you.

NORA (*throws away the tambourine*). You see!

HELMER. I'll have to show you every step.

NORA. You see how much I need you! You must show me every step of the way. Right to the end of the dance. Promise me you will, Torvald?

HELMER. Never fear. I will.

NORA. You mustn't think about anything but me – today or tomorrow. Don't open any letters – don't even open the letter-box –

HELMER. Aha, you're still worried about that fellow –

NORA. Oh, yes, yes, him too.

HELMER. Nora, I can tell from the way you're behaving, there's a letter from him already lying there.

NORA. I don't know. I think so. But you mustn't read it now. I don't want anything ugly to come between us till it's all over.

RANK (*quietly to* HELMER). Better give her her way.

HELMER (*puts his arm round her*). My child shall have her way. But tomorrow night, when your dance is over –

NORA. Then you will be free.

MAID (*appears in the doorway, right*). Dinner is served, madam.

NORA. Put out some champagne, Helen.

MAID. Very good, madam. (*Goes.*)

HELMER. I say! What's this, a banquet?

NORA. We'll drink champagne until dawn! (*Calls.*) And, Helen! Put out some macaroons! Lots of macaroons – for once!

HELMER (*takes her hands in his*). Now, now, now. Don't get so excited. Where's my little songbird, the one I know?

NORA. All right. Go and sit down – and you, too, Dr Rank. I'll be with you in a minute. Christine, you must help me put my hair up.

RANK (*quietly, as they go*). There's nothing wrong, is there? I mean, she isn't – er – expecting – ?

HELMER. Good heavens no, my dear chap. She just gets scared like a child sometimes – I told you before –

They go out, right.

NORA. Well?

MRS LINDE. He's left town.

NORA. I saw it from your face.

MRS LINDE. He'll be back tomorrow evening. I left a note for him.

NORA. You needn't have bothered. You can't stop anything now. Anyway, it's wonderful really, in a way – sitting here and waiting for the miracle to happen.

MRS LINDE. Waiting for what?

NORA. Oh, you wouldn't understand. Go in and join them. I'll be with you in a moment.

> MRS LINDE *goes into the dining-room.*

NORA (*stands for a moment as though collecting herself. Then she looks at her watch*). Five o'clock. Seven hours till midnight. Then another twenty-four hours till midnight tomorrow. And then the tarantella will be finished. Twenty-four and seven? Thirty-one hours to live.

HELMER (*appears in the doorway, right*). What's happened to my little songbird?

NORA (*runs to him with her arms wide*). Your songbird is here!

ACT THREE

The same room. The table which was formerly by the sofa has been moved into the centre of the room; the chairs surround it as before. A lamp is burning on the table. The door to the hall stands open. Dance music can be heard from the floor above. MRS LINDE *is seated at the table, absent-mindedly glancing through a book. She is trying to read, but seems unable to keep her mind on it. More than once she turns and listens anxiously towards the front door.*

MRS LINDE (*looks at her watch*). Not here yet. There's not much time left. Please God he hasn't – ! (*Listens again.*) Ah, here he is.

    Goes out into the hall and cautiously opens the front door. Footsteps can be heard softly ascending the stairs.

MRS LINDE (*whispers*). Come in. There's no one here.

KROGSTAD (*in the doorway*). I found a note from you at my lodgings. What does this mean?

MRS LINDE. I must speak with you.

KROGSTAD. Oh? And must our conversation take place in this house?

MRS LINDE. We couldn't meet at my place; my room has no separate entrance. Come in. We're quite alone. The maid's asleep, and the Helmers are at the dance upstairs.

KROGSTAD (*comes into the room*). Well, well! So the Helmers are dancing this evening? Are they indeed?

MRS LINDE. Yes, why not?

KROGSTAD. True enough. Why not?

MRS LINDE. Well, Krogstad. You and I must have a talk together.

KROGSTAD. Have we two anything further to discuss?

MRS LINDE. We have a great deal to discuss.

KROGSTAD. I wasn't aware of it.

MRS LINDE. That's because you've never really understood me.

KROGSTAD. Was there anything to understand? It's the old story, isn't it – a woman chucking a man because something better turns up?

MRS LINDE. Do you really think I'm so utterly heartless? You think it was easy for me to give you up?

KROGSTAD. Wasn't it?

MRS LINDE. Oh, Nils, did you really believe that?

KROGSTAD. Then why did you write to me the way you did?

MRS LINDE. I had to. Since I had to break with you, I thought it my duty to destroy all the feelings you had for me.

KROGSTAD (*clenches his fists*). So that was it. And you did this for money!

MRS LINDE. You mustn't forget I had a helpless mother to take care of, and two little brothers. We couldn't wait for you, Nils. It would have been so long before you'd have had enough to support us.

KROGSTAD. Maybe. But you had no right to cast me off for someone else.

MRS LINDE. Perhaps not. I've often asked myself that.

KROGSTAD (*more quietly*). When I lost you, it was just as though all solid ground had been swept from under my feet. Look at me. Now I'm a shipwrecked man, clinging to a spar.

MRS LINDE. Help may be near at hand.

KROGSTAD. It was near. But then you came, and stood between it and me.

MRS LINDE. I didn't know, Nils. No one told me till today that this job I'd found was yours.

KROGSTAD. I believe you, since you say so. But now you know, won't you give it up?

MRS LINDE. No – because it wouldn't help you even if I did.

KROGSTAD. Wouldn't it? I'd do it all the same.

MRS LINDE. I've learned to look at things practically. Life and poverty have taught me that.

KROGSTAD. And life has taught me to distrust fine words.

MRS LINDE. Then it has taught you a useful lesson. But surely you still believe in actions?

KROGSTAD. What do you mean?

MRS LINDE. You said you were like a shipwrecked man clinging to a spar.

KROGSTAD. I have good reason to say it.

MRS LINDE. I'm in the same position as you. No one to care about, no one to care for.

KROGSTAD. You made your own choice.

MRS LINDE. I had no choice – then.

KROGSTAD. Well?

MRS LINDE. Nils, suppose we two shipwrecked souls could join hands?

KROGSTAD. What are you saying?

MRS LINDE. Castaways have a better chance of survival together than on their own.

KROGSTAD. Christine!

MRS LINDE. Why do you suppose I came to this town?

KROGSTAD. You mean – you came because of me?

MRS LINDE. I must work if I'm to find life worth living. I've always worked, for as long as I can remember. It's been the greatest joy of my life – my only joy. But now I'm alone in the world, and I feel so dreadfully lost and empty. There's no joy in working just for oneself. Oh, Nils, give me something – someone – to work for.

KROGSTAD. I don't believe all that. You're just being hysterical and romantic. You want to find an excuse for self-sacrifice.

MRS LINDE. Have you ever known me to be hysterical?

KROGSTAD. You mean you really – ? Is it possible? Tell me – you know all about my past?

MRS LINDE. Yes.

KROGSTAD. And you know what people think of me here?

MRS LINDE. You said just now that with me you might have become a different person.

KROGSTAD. I know I could have.

MRS LINDE. Couldn't it still happen?

KROGSTAD. Christine – do you really mean this? Yes – you do – I see it in your face. Have you really the courage – ?

MRS LINDE. I need someone to be a mother to; and your children need a mother. And you and I need each other. I believe in you, Nils. I am afraid of nothing – with you.

KROGSTAD (*clasps her hands*). Thank you, Christine – thank you! Now I shall make the world believe in me as you do! Oh – but I'd forgotten –

MRS LINDE (*listens*). Ssh! The tarantella! Go quickly, go!

KROGSTAD. Why? What is it?

MRS LINDE. You hear that dance? As soon as it's finished, they'll be coming down.

KROGSTAD. All right, I'll go. It's no good, Christine. I'd forgotten – you don't know what I've just done to the Helmers.

MRS LINDE. Yes, Nils. I know.

KROGSTAD. And yet you'd still have the courage to – ?

MRS LINDE. I know what despair can drive a man like you to.

KROGSTAD. Oh, if only I could undo this!

MRS LINDE. You can. Your letter is still lying in the box.

KROGSTAD. Are you sure?

MRS LINDE. Quite sure. But –

KROGSTAD (*looks searchingly at her*). Is that why you're doing this? You want to save your friend at any price? Tell me the truth. Is that the reason?

MRS LINDE. Nils, a woman who has sold herself once for the sake of others doesn't make the same mistake again.

KROGSTAD. I shall demand my letter back.

MRS LINDE. No, no.

KROGSTAD. Of course I shall. I shall stay here till Helmer comes down. I'll tell him he must give me back my letter – I'll say it was only to do with my dismissal, and that I don't want him to read it –

MRS LINDE. No, Nils, you mustn't ask for that letter back.

KROGSTAD. But – tell me – wasn't that the real reason you asked me to come here?

MRS LINDE. Yes – at first, when I was frightened. But a day has passed since then, and in that time I've seen incredible things happen in this house. Helmer must know the truth. This unhappy secret of Nora's must be revealed. They must come to a full understanding. There must be an end of all these shiftings and evasions.

KROGSTAD. Very well. If you're prepared to risk it. But one thing I can do – and at once –

MRS LINDE (*listens*). Hurry! Go, go! The dance is over. We aren't safe here another moment.

KROGSTAD. I'll wait for you downstairs.

MRS LINDE. Yes, do. You can see me home.

KROGSTAD. I've never been so happy in my life before!

He goes out through the front door. The door leading from the room into the hall remains open.

MRS LINDE (*tidies the room a little and gets her hat and coat*). What a change! Oh, what a change! Someone to work for – to live for! A home to bring joy into! I won't let this chance of happiness slip through my fingers. Oh, why don't they come? (*Listens.*) Ah, here they are. I must get my coat on.

She takes her hat and coat. HELMER's *and* NORA's *voices become audible outside. A key is turned in the lock and* HELMER *leads* NORA *almost forcibly into the hall. She is dressed in an Italian costume with a large black shawl. He is in evening dress, with a black coat.*

NORA (*still in the doorway, resisting him*). No, no, no – not in here! I want to go back upstairs. I don't want to leave so early.

HELMER. But my dearest Nora –

NORA. Oh, please, Torvald, please! Just another hour!

HELMER. Not another minute, Nora, my sweet. You know what we agreed. Come along, now. Into the drawing-room. You'll catch cold if you stay out here.

He leads her, despite her efforts to resist him, gently into the room.

MRS LINDE. Good evening.

NORA. Christine!

HELMER. Oh, hullo, Mrs Linde. You still here?

MRS LINDE. Please forgive me. I did so want to see Nora in her costume.

NORA. Have you been sitting here waiting for me?

MRS LINDE. Yes. I got here too late, I'm afraid. You'd already gone up. And I felt I really couldn't go home without seeing you.

HELMER (*takes off Nora's shawl*). Well, take a good look at her. She's worth looking at, don't you think? Isn't she beautiful, Mrs Linde?

MRS LINDE. Oh, yes, indeed –

HELMER. Isn't she unbelievably beautiful? Everyone at the party said so. But dreadfully stubborn she is, bless her pretty little heart. What's to be done about that? Would you believe it, I practically had to use force to get her away!

NORA. Oh, Torvald, you're going to regret not letting me stay – just half an hour longer.

HELMER. Hear that, Mrs Linde? She dances her tarantella – makes a roaring success – and very well deserved – though possibly a trifle too realistic – more so than was aesthetically necessary, strictly speaking. But never mind that. Main thing is – she had a success – roaring success. Was I going to let her stay on after that and spoil the impression? No, thank you! I took my beautiful little Capri signorina – my capricious little Capricienne, what? – under my arm – a swift round of the ballroom, a curtsy to the company, and, as they say in novels, the beautiful apparition disappeared! An exit should always be dramatic, Mrs Linde. But unfortunately that's just what I can't get Nora to realize. I say, it's hot in here. (*Throws his cloak on a chair and opens the door to his study.*) What's this? It's dark in here. Ah, yes, of course – excuse me. (*Goes in and lights a couple of candles.*)

NORA (*whispers softly, breathlessly*). Well?

MRS LINDE (*quietly*). I've spoken to him.

NORA. Yes?

MRS LINDE. Nora – you must tell your husband everything.

NORA (*dully*). I knew it.

MRS LINDE. You have nothing to fear from Krogstad. But you must tell him.

NORA. I shan't tell him anything.

MRS LINDE. Then the letter will.

NORA. Thank you, Christine. Now I know what I must do. Ssh!

HELMER (*returns*). Well, Mrs Linde, finished admiring her?

MRS LINDE. Yes. Now I must say good night.

HELMER. Oh, already? Does this knitting belong to you?

MRS LINDE (*takes it*). Thank you, yes. I nearly forgot it.

HELMER. You knit, then?

MRS LINDE. Why, yes.

HELMER. Know what? You ought to take up embroidery.

MRS LINDE. Oh? Why?

HELMER. It's much prettier. Watch me, now. You hold the embroidery in your left hand, like this, and then you take the needle in your right hand and go in and out in a slow, easy movement – like this. I am right, aren't I?

MRS LINDE. Yes, I'm sure –

HELMER. But knitting, now – that's an ugly business – can't help it. Look – arms all huddled up – great clumsy needles going up and down – makes you look like a damned Chinaman. I say that really was a magnificent champagne they served us.

MRS LINDE. Well, good night, Nora. And stop being stubborn! Remember!

HELMER. Quite right, Mrs Linde!

MRS LINDE. Good night, Mr Helmer.

HELMER (*accompanies her to the door*). Good night, good night!

I hope you'll manage to get home all right? I'd gladly – but you haven't far to go, have you? Good night, good night.

She goes. He closes the door behind her and returns.

HELMER. Well, we've got rid of her at last. Dreadful bore that woman is!

NORA. Aren't you very tired, Torvald?

HELMER. No, not in the least.

NORA. Aren't you sleepy?

HELMER. Not a bit. On the contrary, I feel extraordinary exhilarated. But what about you? Yes, you look very sleepy and tired.

NORA. Yes, I am very tired. Soon I shall sleep.

HELMER. You see, you see! How right I was not to let you stay longer!

NORA. Oh, you're always right, whatever you do.

HELMER (*kisses her on the forehead*). Now my little songbird's talking just like a real big human being. I say, did you notice how cheerful Rank was this evening?

NORA. Oh? Was he? I didn't have a chance to speak with him.

HELMER. I hardly did. But I haven't seen him in such a jolly mood for ages. (*Looks at her for a moment, then comes closer.*) I say, it's nice to get back to one's home again, and be all alone with you. Upon my word, you're a distractingly beautiful young woman.

NORA. Don't look at me like that, Torvald!

HELMER. What, not look at my most treasured possession? At all this wonderful beauty that's mine, mine alone, all mine.

NORA (*goes round to the other side of the table*). You mustn't talk to me like that tonight.

HELMER (*follows her*). You've still the tarantella in your blood, I see. And that makes you even more desirable. Listen! Now the other guests are beginning to go. (*More quietly.*) Nora – soon the whole house will be absolutely quiet.

NORA. Yes, I hope so.

HELMER. Yes, my beloved Nora, of course you do! You know – when I'm out with you among other people like we were tonight, do you know why I say so little to you, why I keep so aloof from you, and just throw you an occasional glance? Do you know why I do that? It's because I pretend to myself that you're my secret mistress, my clandestine little sweetheart, and that nobody knows there's anything at all between us.

NORA. Oh, yes, yes, yes – I know you never think of anything but me.

HELMER. And then when we're about to go, and I wrap the shawl round your lovely young shoulders, over this wonderful curve of your neck – then I pretend to myself that you are my young bride, that we've just come from the wedding, that I'm taking you to my house for the first time – that, for the first time, I am alone with you – quite alone with you, as you stand there young and trembling and beautiful. All evening I've had no eyes for anyone but you. When I saw you dance the tarantella, like a huntress, a temptress, my blood grew hot, I couldn't stand it any longer! That was why I seized you and dragged you down here with me –

NORA. Leave me, Torvald! Get away from me! I don't want all this.

HELMER. What? Now, Nora, you're joking with me. Don't want, don't want – ? Aren't I your husband?

There is a knock on the front door.

NORA (*starts*). What was that?

HELMER (*goes towards the hall*). Who is it?

DR RANK (*outside*). It's me. May I come in for a moment?

HELMER (*quietly, annoyed*). Oh, what does he want now? (*Calls.*) Wait a moment. (*Walks over and opens the door.*) Well! Nice of you not to go by without looking in.

RANK. I thought I heard your voice, so I felt I had to say goodbye. (*His eyes travel swiftly around the room.*) Ah, yes – these dear rooms, how well I know them. What a happy, peaceful home you two have.

HELMER. You seemed to be having a pretty happy time yourself upstairs.

RANK. Indeed I did. Why not? Why shouldn't one make the most of this world? As much as one can, and for as long as one can. The wine was excellent –

HELMER. Especially the champagne.

RANK. You noticed that too? It's almost incredible how much I managed to get down.

NORA. Torvald drank a lot of champagne too, this evening.

RANK. Oh?

NORA. Yes. It always makes him merry afterwards.

RANK. Well, why shouldn't a man have a merry evening after a well-spent day?

HELMER. Well-spent? Oh, I don't know that I can claim that.

RANK (slaps him across the back). I can, though, my dear fellow!

NORA. Yes, of course, Dr Rank – you've been carrying out a scientific experiment today, haven't you?

RANK. Exactly.

HELMER. Scientific experiment! Those are big words for my little Nora to use!

NORA. And may I congratulate you on the finding?

RANK. You may indeed.

NORA. It was good then?

RANK. The best possible finding – both for the doctor and the patient. Certainty.

NORA (quickly). Certainty?

RANK. Absolute certainty. So aren't I entitled to have a merry evening after that?

NORA. Yes, Dr Rank. You were quite right to.

HELMER. I agree. Provided you don't have to regret it tomorrow.

RANK. Well, you never get anything in this life without paying for it.

NORA. Dr Rank – you like masquerades, don't you?

RANK. Yes, if the disguises are sufficiently amusing.

NORA. Tell me. What shall we two wear at the next masquerade?

HELMER. You little gadabout! Are you thinking about the next one already?

RANK. We two? Yes, I'll tell you. You must go as the Spirit of Happiness –

HELMER. You try to think of a costume that'll convey that.

RANK. Your wife need only appear as her normal, everyday self –

HELMER. Quite right! Well said! But what are you going to be? Have you decided that?

RANK. Yes, my dear friend. I have decided that.

HELMER. Well?

RANK. At the next masquerade, I shall be invisible.

HELMER. Well, that's a funny idea.

RANK. There's a big, black hat – haven't you heard of the invisible hat? Once it's over your head, no one can see you any more.

HELMER (*represses a smile*). Ah yes, of course.

RANK. But I'm forgetting what I came for. Helmer, give me a cigar. One of your black Havanas.

HELMER. With the greatest pleasure. (*Offers him the box.*)

RANK (*takes one and cuts off the tip*). Thank you.

NORA (*strikes a match*). Let me give you a light.

RANK. Thank you. (*She holds out the match for him. He lights his cigar.*) And now – goodbye.

HELMER. Goodbye, my dear chap, goodbye.

NORA. Sleep well, Dr Rank.

RANK. Thank you for that kind wish.

NORA. Wish me the same.

RANK. You? Very well – since you ask. Sleep well. And thank you for the light. (*He nods to them both and goes.*)

HELMER (*quietly*). He's been drinking too much.

NORA (*abstractedly*). Perhaps.

HELMER *takes his bunch of keys from his pocket and goes out into the hall.*

NORA. Torvald, what do you want out there?

HELMER. I must empty the letter-box. It's absolutely full. There'll be no room for the newspapers in the morning.

NORA. Are you going to work tonight?

HELMER. You know very well I'm not. Hullo, what's this? Someone's been at the lock.

NORA. At the lock –

HELMER. Yes, I'm sure of it. Who on earth – ? Surely not one of the maids? Here's a broken hairpin. Nora, it's yours –

NORA (*quickly*). Then it must have been the children.

HELMER. Well, you'll have to break them of that habit. Hm, hm. Ah, that's done it. (*Takes out the contents of the box and calls into the kitchen.*) Helen! Helen! Put out the light on the staircase. (*Comes back into the drawing-room and closes the door to the hall.*)

HELMER (*with the letters in his hand*). Look at this! You see how they've piled up? (*Glances through them.*) What on earth's this?

NORA (*at the window*). The letter! Oh no, Torvald, no!

HELMER. Two visiting cards – from Rank.

NORA. From Dr Rank?

HELMER (*looks at them*). Peter Rank, M.D. They were on top. He must have dropped them in as he left.

NORA. Has he written anything on them?

HELMER. There's a black cross above his name. Rather gruesome, isn't it? It looks just as thought he was announcing his death.

NORA. He is.

HELMER. What? Do you know something? Has he told you anything?

NORA. Yes. When these cards come, it means he's said goodbye to us. He wants to shut himself up in his house and die.

HELMER. Ah, poor fellow. I knew I wouldn't be seeing him for much longer. But so soon – ! And now he's going to slink away and hide like a wounded beast.

NORA. When the time comes, it's best to go silently. Don't you think so, Torvald?

HELMER (*walks up and down*). He was so much a part of our life. I can't realize that he's gone. His suffering and loneliness seemed to provide a kind of dark background to the happy sunlight of our marriage. Well, perhaps it's best this way. For him, anyway. (*Stops walking.*) And perhaps for us too, Nora.

Now we have only each other. (*Embraces her.*) Oh, my beloved wife – I feel as though I could never hold you close enough. Do you know, Nora, often I wish some terrible danger might threaten you, so that I could offer my life and my blood, everything, for your sake.

NORA (*tears herself loose and says in a clear, firm voice*). Read your letters now, Torvald.

HELMER. No, no. Not tonight. Tonight I want to be with you, my darling wife –

NORA. When your friend is about to die – ?

HELMER. You're right. This news has upset us both. An ugliness has come between us; thoughts of death and dissolution. We must try to forget them. Until then – you go to your room; I shall go to mine.

NORA (*throws her arms round his neck*). Good night, Torvald! Good night!

HELMER (*kisses her on the forehead*). Good night, my darling little songbird. Sleep well, Nora. I'll go and read my letters.

He goes into the study with the letters in his hand, and closes the door.

NORA (*wild-eyed, fumbles around, seizes* HELMER's *cloak, throws it round herself and whispers quickly, hoarsely*). Never see him again. Never. Never. Never. (*Throws the shawl over her head.*) Never see the children again. Them, too. Never. Never. Oh – the icy black water! Oh – that bottomless – that – ! Oh, if only it were all over! Now he's got it – he's reading it. Oh no, no! Not yet! Goodbye Torvald! Goodbye my darlings!

She turns to run into the hall. As she does so, HELMER *throws open his door and stands there with an open letter in his hand.*

HELMER. Nora!

NORA (*shrieks*). Ah – !

HELMER. What is this? Do you know what is in this letter?

NORA. Yes, I know. Let me go! Let me go!

HELMER (*holding her back*). Go? Where?

NORA (*tries to tear herself loose*). You mustn't try to save me, Torvald!

HELMER (*staggers back*). Is it true? Is it true, what he writes? Oh, my God! No, no – it's impossible, it can't be true!

NORA. It *is* true. I've loved you more than anything else in the world.

HELMER. Oh, don't try to make silly excuses.

NORA (*takes a step towards him*). Torvald –

HELMER. Wretched woman! What have you done?

NORA. Let me go! You're not going to suffer for my sake. I won't let you!

HELMER. Stop being theatrical. (*Locks the front door.*) You're going to stay here and explain yourself. Do you understand what you've done? Answer me! Do you understand?

NORA (*looks unflinchingly at him and, her expression growing colder, says*). Yes. Now I am beginning to understand.

HELMER (*walking round the room*). Oh, what a dreadful awakening! For eight whole years – she who was my joy and pride – a hypocrite, a liar – worse, worse – a criminal! Oh, the hideousness of it! Shame on you, shame!

NORA *is silent and stares unblinkingly at him.*

HELMER (*stops in front of her*). I ought to have guessed that something of this sort would happen. I should have foreseen it. All your father's recklessness and instability – be quiet! – I repeat, all your father's recklessness and instability he has handed on to you! No religion, no morals, no sense of duty! Oh, how I have been punished for closing my eyes to his faults! I did it for your sake. And now you reward me like this.

NORA. Yes. Like this.

HELMER. Now you have destroyed all my happiness. You have ruined my whole future. Oh, it's too dreadful to contemplate! I am in the power of a man who is completely without scruples. He can do what he likes with me, demand what he pleases, order me to do anything – I dare not disobey him. I am condemned to humiliation and ruin simply for the weakness of a woman.

NORA. When I am gone from this world, you will be free.

HELMER. Oh, don't be melodramatic. Your father was always ready with that kind of remark. How would it help me if you were 'gone from this world', as you put it? It wouldn't assist me in the slightest. He can still make all the facts public; and if he does, I may quite easily be suspected of having been an accomplice in your crime. People may think that I was behind it – that it was I who encouraged you! And for all this I have to thank you, you whom I have carried on my hands through all the years of our marriage! Now do you realize what you've done to me?

NORA (*coldly calm*). Yes.

HELMER. It's so unbelievable I can hardly credit it. But we must try to find some way out. Take off that shawl. Take it off, I say! I must try to buy him off somehow. This thing must be hushed up at any price. As regards our relationship – we must appear to be living together just as before. Only *appear*, of course. You will therefore continue to reside here. That is understood. But the children shall be taken out of your hands. I dare no longer entrust them to you. Oh, to have to say this to the woman I once loved so dearly – and whom I still – ! Well, all that must be finished. Henceforth there can be no question of happiness; we must merely strive to save what shreds and tatters –

The front door bell rings. HELMER *starts.*

HELMER. What can that be? At this hour? Surely not – ? He wouldn't – ? Hide yourself, Nora. Say you're ill.

NORA *does not move.* HELMER *goes to the door of the room and opens it. The* MAID *is standing half-dressed in the hall.*

MAID. A letter for madam.

HELMER. Give it me. (*Seizes the letter and shuts the door.*) Yes, it's from him. You're not having it. I'll read this myself.

NORA. Read it.

HELMER (*by the lamp*). I hardly dare to. This may mean the end

for us both. No. I must know. (*Tears open the letter hastily;
reads a few lines; looks at a piece of paper which is enclosed with it;
utters a cry of joy.*) Nora! (*She looks at him questioningly.*) Nora!
No – I must read it once more. Yes, yes, it's true! I am saved!
Nora, I am saved!

NORA. What about me?

HELMER. You too, of course. We're both saved, you and I. Look!
He's returning your I.O.U. He writes that he is sorry for what
has happened – a happy accident has changed his life – oh,
what does it matter what he writes? We are saved, Nora! No
one can harm you now. Oh, Nora, Nora – no, first let me destroy
this filthy thing. Let me see – ! (*Glances at the I.O.U.*) No, I
don't want to look at it. I shall merely regard the whole business
as a dream. (*He tears the I.O.U. and both letters into pieces,
throws them into the stove and watches them burn.*) There. Now
they're destroyed. He wrote that ever since Christmas Eve
you've been – oh, these must have been three dreadful days for
you, Nora.

NORA. Yes. It's been a hard fight.

HELMER. It must have been terrible – seeing no way out except –
no, we'll forget the whole sordid business. We'll just be happy
and go on telling ourselves over and over again: 'It's over!
It's over!' Listen to me, Nora. You don't seem to realize. It's
over! Why are you looking so pale? Ah, my poor little Nora, I
understand. You can't believe that I have forgiven you. But I
have, Nora. I swear it to you. I have forgiven you everything.
I know that what you did you did for your love of me.

NORA. That is true.

HELMER. You have loved me as a wife should love her husband.
It was simply that in your inexperience you chose the wrong
means. But do you think I love you any the less because you
don't know how to act on your own initiative? No, no. Just lean
on me. I shall counsel you. I shall guide you. I would not be a
true man if your feminine helplessness did not make you doubly
attractive in my eyes. You mustn't mind the hard words I said

to you in those first dreadful moments when my whole world seemed to be tumbling about my ears. I have forgiven you, Nora. I swear it to you; I have forgiven you.

NORA. Thank you for your forgiveness. (*She goes out through the door, right.*)

HELMER. No, don't go – (*Looks in.*) What are you doing there?

NORA (*offstage*). Taking off my fancy dress.

HELMER (*by the open door*). Yes, do that. Try to calm yourself and get your balance again, my frightened little songbird. Don't be afraid. I have broad wings to shield you. (*Begins to walk around near the door.*) How lovely and peaceful this little home of ours is, Nora. You are safe here; I shall watch over you like a hunted dove which I have snatched unharmed from the claws of the falcon. Your wildly beating little heart shall find peace with me. It will happen, Nora; it will take time, but it will happen, believe me. Tomorrow all this will seem quite different. Soon everything will be as it was before. I shall no longer need to remind you that I have forgiven you; your own heart will tell you that it is true. Do you really think I could ever bring myself to disown you, or even to reproach you? Ah, Nora, you don't understand what goes on in a husband's heart. There is something indescribably wonderful and satisfying for a husband in knowing that he has forgiven his wife – forgiven her unreservedly, from the bottom of his heart. It means that she has become his property in a double sense; he has, as it were, brought her into the world anew; she is now not only his wife but also his child. From now on that is what you shall be to me, my poor, helpless, bewildered little creature. Never be frightened of anything again, Nora. Just open your heart to me. I shall be both your will and your conscience. What's this? Not in bed? Have you changed?

NORA (*in her everyday dress*). Yes, Torvald. I've changed.

HELMER. But why now – so late – ?

NORA. I shall not sleep tonight.

HELMER. But, my dear Nora –

NORA (*looks at her watch*). It isn't that late. Sit down there, Torvald. You and I have a lot to talk about.

She sits down on one side of the table.

HELMER. Nora, what does this mean? You look quite drawn –

NORA. Sit down. It's going to take a long time. I've a lot to say to you.

HELMER (*sits down on the other side of the table*). You alarm me, Nora. I don't understand you.

NORA. No, that's just it. You don't understand me. And I've never understood you – until this evening. No, don't interrupt me. Just listen to what I have to say. You and I have got to face facts, Torvald.

HELMER. What do you mean by that?

NORA (*after a short silence*). Doesn't anything strike you about the way we're sitting here?

HELMER. What?

NORA. We've been married for eight years. Does it occur to you that this is the first time we two, you and I, man and wife, have ever had a serious talk together?

HELMER. Serious? What do you mean, serious?

NORA. In eight whole years – no, longer – ever since we first met – we have never exchanged a serious word on a serious subject.

HELMER. Did you expect me to drag you into all my worries – worries you couldn't possibly have helped me with?

NORA. I'm not talking about worries. I'm simply saying that we have never sat down seriously to try to get to the bottom of anything.

HELMER. But, my dear Nora, what on earth has that got to do with you?

NORA. That's just the point. You have never understood me. A great wrong has been done to me, Torvald. First by papa, and then by you.

HELMER. What? But we two have loved you more than anyone in the world!

NORA (*shakes her head*). You have never loved me. You just thought it was fun to be in love with me.

HELMER. Nora, what kind of a way is this to talk?

NORA. It's the truth, Torvald. When I lived with papa, he used to tell me what he thought about everything, so that I never had any opinions but his. And if I did have any of my own, I kept them quiet, because he wouldn't have liked them. He called me his little doll, and he played with me just the way I played with my dolls. Then I came here to live in your house –

HELMER. What kind of a way is that to describe our marriage?

NORA (*undisturbed*). I mean, then I passed from papa's hands into yours. You arranged everything the way you wanted it, so that I simply took over your taste in everything – or pretended I did – I don't really know – I think it was a little of both – first one and then the other. Now I look back on it, it's as if I've been living here like a pauper, from hand to mouth. I performed tricks for you, and you gave me food and drink. But that was how you wanted it. You and papa have done me a great wrong. It's your fault that I have done nothing with my life.

HELMER. Nora, how can you be so unreasonable and ungrateful? Haven't you been happy here?

NORA. No; never. I used to think I was. But I haven't ever been happy.

HELMER. Not – not happy?

NORA. No. I've just had fun. You've always been very kind to me. But our home has never been anything but a playroom. I've been your doll-wife, just as I used to be papa's doll-child. And the children have been my dolls. I used to think it was fun when you came in and played with me, just as they think it's fun when I go in and play games with them. That's all our marriage has been, Torvald.

HELMER. There may be a little truth in what you say, though you exaggerate and romanticize. But from now on it'll be different. Playtime is over. Now the time has come for education.

NORA. Whose education? Mine or the children's?

HELMER. Both yours and the children's, my dearest Nora.

NORA. Oh, Torvald, you're not the man to educate me into being the right wife for you.

HELMER. How can you say that?

NORA. And what about me? Am I fit to educate the children?

HELMER. Nora!

NORA. Didn't you say yourself a few minutes ago that you dare not leave them in my charge?

HELMER. In a moment of excitement. Surely you don't think I meant it seriously?

NORA. Yes. You were perfectly right. I'm not fitted to educate them. There's something else I must do first. I must educate myself. And you can't help me with that. It's something I must do by myself. That's why I'm leaving you.

HELMER (*jumps up*). What did you say?

NORA. I must stand on my own feet if I am to find out the truth about myself and about life. So I can't go on living here with you any longer.

HELMER. Nora, Nora!

NORA. I'm leaving you now, at once. Christine will put me up for tonight –

HELMER. You're out of your mind! You can't do this! I forbid you!

NORA. It's no use your trying to forbid me any more. I shall take with me nothing but what is mine. I don't want anything from you, now or ever.

HELMER. What kind of madness is this?

NORA. Tomorrow I shall go home – I mean, to where I was born. It'll be easiest for me to find some kind of a job there.

HELMER. But you're blind! You've no experience of the world –

NORA. I must try to get some, Torvald.

HELMER. But to leave your home, your husband, your children! Have you thought what people will say?

NORA. I can't help that. I only know that I must do this.

HELMER. But this is monstrous! Can you neglect your most sacred duties?

NORA. What do you call my most sacred duties?

HELMER. Do I have to tell you? Your duties towards your husband, and your children.

NORA. I have another duty which is equally sacred.

HELMER. You have not. What on earth could that be?

NORA. My duty towards myself.

HELMER. First and foremost you are a wife and mother.

NORA. I don't believe that any longer. I believe that I am first and foremost a human being, like you – or anyway, that I must try to become one. I know most people think as you do, Torvald, and I know there's something of the sort to be found in books. But I'm no longer prepared to accept what people say and what's written in books. I must think things out for myself, and try to find my own answer.

HELMER. Do you need to ask where your duty lies in your own home? Haven't you an infallible guide in such matters – your religion?

NORA. Oh, Torvald, I don't really know what religion means.

HELMER. What are you saying?

NORA. I only know what Pastor Hansen told me when I went to confirmation. He explained that religion meant this and that. When I get away from all this and can think things out on my own, that's one of the questions I want to look into. I want to find out whether what Pastor Hansen said was right – or anyway, whether it is right for me.

HELMER. But it's unheard of for so young a woman to behave like this! If religion cannot guide you, let me at least appeal to your conscience. I presume you have some moral feelings left? Or – perhaps you haven't? Well, answer me.

NORA. Oh, Torvald, that isn't an easy question to answer. I simply don't know. I don't know where I am in these matters. I only know that these things mean something quite different to me from what they do to you. I've learned now that certain laws are different from what I'd imagined them to be; but I can't accept that such laws can be right. Has a woman really not the right to spare her dying father pain, or save her husband's life? I can't believe that.

HELMER. You're talking like a child. You don't understand how society works.

NORA. No, I don't. But now I intend to learn. I must try to satisfy myself which is right, society or I.

HELMER. Nora, you're ill. You're feverish. I almost believe you're out of your mind.

NORA. I've never felt so sane and sure in my life.

HELMER. You feel sure that it is right to leave your husband and your children?

NORA. Yes. I do.

HELMER. Then there is only one possible explanation.

NORA. What?

HELMER. That you don't love me any longer.

NORA. No, that's exactly it.

HELMER. Nora! How can you say this to me?

NORA. Oh, Torvald, it hurts me terribly to have to say it, because you've always been so kind to me. But I can't help it. I don't love you any longer.

HELMER (*controlling his emotions with difficulty*). And you feel quite sure about this, too?

NORA. Yes, absolutely sure. That's why I can't go on living here any longer.

HELMER. Can you also explain why I have lost your love?

NORA. Yes, I can. It happened this evening, when the miracle failed to happen. It was then that I realized you weren't the man I'd thought you to be.

HELMER. Explain more clearly. I don't understand you.

NORA. I've waited so patiently, for eight whole years – well, good heavens, I'm not such a fool as to suppose that miracles occur every day. Then this dreadful thing happened to me, and then I *knew*: 'Now the miracle will take place!' When Krogstad's letter was lying out there, it never occurred to me for a moment that you would let that man trample over you. I *knew* that you would say to him: 'Publish the facts to the world!' And when he had done this –

HELMER. Yes, what then? When I'd exposed my wife's name to shame and scandal –

NORA. Then I was certain that you would step forward and take all the blame on yourself, and say: 'I am the one who is guilty!'

HELMER. Nora!

NORA. You're thinking I wouldn't have accepted such a sacrifice from you? No, of course I wouldn't! But what would my word have counted for against yours? That was the miracle I was hoping for, and dreading. And it was to prevent it happening that I wanted to end my life.

HELMER. Nora, I would gladly work for you night and day, and endure sorrow and hardship for your sake. But no man can be expected to sacrifice his honour, even for the person he loves.

NORA. Millions of women have done it.

HELMER. Oh, you think and talk like a stupid child.

NORA. That may be. But you neither think nor talk like the man I could share my life with. Once you'd got over your fright – and you weren't frightened of what might threaten me, but only of what threatened you – once the danger was past, then as far as you were concerned it was exactly as though nothing had happened. I was your little songbird just as before – your doll whom henceforth you would take particular care to protect from the world because she was so weak and fragile. (*Gets up.*) Torvald, in that moment I realized that for eight years I had been living here with a complete stranger, and had borne him three children – ! Oh, I can't bear to think of it! I could tear myself to pieces!

HELMER (*sadly*). I see it, I see it. A gulf has indeed opened between us. Oh, but Nora – couldn't it be bridged?

NORA. As I am now, I am no wife for you.

HELMER. I have the strength to change.

NORA. Perhaps – if your doll is taken from you.

HELMER. But to be parted – to be parted from you! No, no, Nora, I can't conceive of it happening!

NORA (*goes into the room, right*). All the more necessary that it should happen.

She comes back with her outdoor things and a small travelling-bag, which she puts down on a chair by the table.

HELMER. Nora, Nora, not now! Wait till tomorrow!

NORA (*puts on her coat*). I can't spend the night in a strange man's house.

HELMER. But can't we live here as brother and sister, then – ?

NORA (*fastens her hat*). You know quite well it wouldn't last. (*Puts on her shawl.*) Goodbye, Torvald. I don't want to see the children. I know they're in better hands than mine. As I am now, I can be nothing to them.

HELMER. But some time, Nora – some time – ?

NORA. How can I tell? I've no idea what will happen to me.

HELMER. But you are my wife, both as you are and as you will be.

NORA. Listen, Torvald. When a wife leaves her husband's house, as I'm doing now, I'm told that according to the law he is freed of any obligations towards her. In any case, I release you from any such obligations. You mustn't feel bound to me in any way however small, just as I shall not feel bound to you. We must both be quite free. Here is your ring back. Give me mine.

HELMER. That too?

NORA. That too.

HELMER. Here it is.

NORA. Good. Well, now it's over. I'll leave the keys here. The servants know about everything to do with the house – much better than I do. Tomorrow, when I have left town, Christine will come to pack the things I brought here from home. I'll have them sent on after me.

HELMER. This is the end, then! Nora, will you never think of me any more?

NORA. Yes, of course. I shall often think of you and the children and this house.

HELMER. May I write to you, Nora?

NORA. No. Never. You mustn't do that.

HELMER. But at least you must let me send you –

NORA. Nothing. Nothing.

HELMER. But if you should need help – ?

NORA. I tell you, no. I don't accept things from strangers.

HELMER. Nora – can I never be anything but a stranger to you?

NORA (*picks up her bag*). Oh, Torvald! Then the miracle of miracles would have to happen.

HELMER. The miracle of miracles!

NORA. You and I would both have to change so much that – oh, Torvald, I don't believe in miracles any longer.

HELMER. But I want to believe in them. Tell me. We should have to change so much that – !

NORA. That life together between us two could become a marriage. Goodbye.

She goes out through the hall.

HELMER (*sinks down on a chair by the door and buries his face in his hands*). Nora! Nora! (*Looks round and gets up.*) Empty! She's gone! (*A hope strikes him.*) The miracle of miracles – ?

The street door is slammed shut downstairs.

Note on the Translation

A Doll's House presents fewer problems to the translator than any other of Ibsen's plays, except perhaps *An Enemy of the People*. It is simply and directly written, and for nearly all the time the characters say what they mean, instead of talking at a tangent to their real meaning. Torvald Helmer utters several stuffy Victorianisms, and Krogstad sometimes speaks the language of melodrama, but both work well in performance. Here, as in all the plays, I have retained certain turns of phrase which look Victorian on the printed page but are effective in the theatre when spoken by an actor or actress in nineteenth-century clothes in a nineteenth-century room.

Notes

Act One

23 *a stove lined with porcelain tiles* — a familiar item of
furniture in countries such as Norway before the age of central
heating. The stove usually stood against a wall, sometimes
extending as high as the ceiling, and was decoratively ornamented
with glazed tiles on the outside which also retained and gave off
heat. A door in front could be opened to feed the stove, which was
usually fuelled with wood.

23 *a what-not* — article of furniture consisting of an open stand
with shelves one above another, for keeping or displaying objects.

23 *A bell rings* — unlike Helmer, Nora seems not to carry a front
door key.

23 *Here's a pound* — a confident act of generosity which
anticipates Helmer's accusations of being a squanderer. The fact that
Nora is carrying 'a lot of parcels' also helps to define her attitude
towards money.

23 *macaroons* — small cakes or biscuits made of ground
almonds, white of egg, sugar etc.

24 *see what I've bought* — despite asking not to be disturbed,
Helmer appears at the mention of money being spent.

25 *Who cares about them? They're strangers* — a very selfish
and immature attitude which anticipates her response to Dr.
Rank's announcement of his state of health.

25 *how like a woman!* — such remarks speak volumes about
Helmer's 'sexist' attitudes.

25 *A home that is founded on debts and borrowing can never
be a place of freedom and beauty* — a pretentiously sonorous
phrase which ensures that the audience knows very early on what
Helmer's attitude is on this crucial point.

25 *And some bits of material and handkerchiefs for the maids* —
Nora's generosity would seem to extend only to her own kind.

26 *I save every penny I can* — it transpires that she does but, at
this point, an audience is more likely to believe Helmer's
estimation of Nora simply because of the evidence before them.

27 *But there's no need; he knows he'll be dining with us* —

Rank's position within the household is well-established.

28   *Yes, it's almost like a miracle* — the first mention of the term which is going to loom so large later in the play.

28   *For three whole weeks* — it is some time before the audience are given the true explanation of what Nora was doing. Such gradual and involved revelations are intrinsic to Ibsen's dramatic method.

28   *Someone's coming. What a bore* — typical of the Helmers' attitude towards outsiders (c.f. Helmer's attitude to Mrs. Linde and Rank pp.87-8).

28   *Has he gone to my room?* — Helmer's study has a separate entrance in the hall, apart from the one in the living-room.

30   *Manager of the bank* — not a large clearing bank like Barclays but more on the lines of a savings bank.

30   *heaps and heaps of money* — (c.f. 'lots and lots of money' p.24.) The image creates a picture of piled up bank notes which in turn, given Nora's equation with the 'squirrel', conjures up the idea of money as piles of dry leaves from which the squirrel makes its drey.

30   *Nora, Nora, haven't you grown up yet?* — Mrs. Linde's smiling patronage seems entirely justified at this point. It forms the necessary and credible stimulus which provokes Nora to reveal 'the truth'.

30   *Wags her finger* — a kind of conscious parody which indicates that she already sees Helmer in a certain light.

32   *Sits on a footstool and rests her arms on Mrs. Linde's knee* — the conventional pose for a schoolgirl confiding her secrets.

33   *tosses her head and walks across the room* — such movements are a reflection of Nora's personality. She moves around restlessly as if confined unwillingly within her environment but tosses her head as if in defiance of those who would regard her as a little pet animal.

34   *the big thing* — such phrases are normally part of a child's vocabulary.

34   *Two hundred and fifty pounds* — A comparatively large sum for the period.

35   *it was his duty as a husband* — Nora is fully aware of Helmer's view of his own role and has attempted to exploit it.

36   *quarterly instalments and interest* — Nora has to repay the loan itself plus the percentage charged as interest on it, at three-monthly intervals.

37   *But it was great fun . . . almost like being a man* — Nora's attitude to a type of routine office work that would normally be regarded as drudgery exemplifies her essentially romantic view of a man's lifestyle.

39 *de trop* — literally 'too much'. Rank feels he is intruding since Nora is entertaining Mrs. Linde.

39 *I believe I passed you on the stairs as I came up* — the first indication that the apartment is not at ground level, a siting which is always significant in Ibsen. The fact that the stairs 'tire' Mrs. Linde, the idealist searching for a reason to live, is also significant.

40 *I find it very amusing to think that we — I mean, Torvald —* a Freudian slip revealing that Nora thinks she wields power through her ability to manipulate Helmer.

40 *Takes the paper bag from her pocket* — a symbolic scorning of Helmer's power and authority.

41 *So when she heard you'd become head of the bank — it was in her local paper* — Nora invents details to clothe her misrepresentation of the facts with smooth ease.

42 *claps her hands* — a characteristic gesture which reduces in frequency as Nora begins to realise the full horror of her position.

43 *throws them anywhere* — Nora is accustomed to servants who tidy up after her. She simply enjoys herself.

43 *. . . dogs don't bite lovely little baby dolls* — Nora's maternalism is underlined as being merely a game.

45 *How dare you presume to cross-examine me* — she attempts to stand on her dignity, falling easily into the uppish tones of a future bank manager's wife.

45 *one . . . one . . . one* — Nora adopts the formal impersonal pronoun in an attempt to sound imposing and intimidate Krogstad.

46 *How on earth could you imagine that I would have any influence over my husband* — she has already demonstrated her power to manipulate him to the audience. She seeks to present Helmer as the strong, efficient paragon expected to fill the post of bank manager.

47 *security for the debt* — Nora's father would repay the debt if she defaulted on the repayments.

48 *Here your father has dated his signature* — Nora didn't even think of giving a false date on the IOU.

48 *The words 'second of October'* — Neither did she, foolishly in the circumstances, attempt to forge his signature. Therefore, she is only a criminal in law and not one in motive. Her dishonesty, which manifests itself frequently, is that of a child.

49 *throws her head back and looks defiantly at him* — Nora exhibits a childish defiance in stating the truth when a lie would have been more appropriate

52   *the trustees* — the Board of Advisers which has the authority to run the bank on behalf of its investors.

52   *slowly strokes the back of his head* — the lead-in, via the red-herring of the dress, to getting Krogstad reinstated.

54   *Lays his hand on her head* — the gesture of blessing of a patriarch.

Act Two

55   *Nothing in the letter-box* — the first reference to the letter-box, a glass container fitted to the inside of the front door to catch the mail and which Ibsen uses to heighten tension in the traditional manner of a 'well-made play'. The letter which Krogstad delivers on p.72 is not opened until p.92.

55   *from now on I shan't be able to spend so much time with them* — Nora accepts the validity of Helmer's opinion on the 'poisoning' her children, c.f. p.53.

56   *That good-for-nothing* — it is noticeable that Anne-Marie only blames the father of her child. She accepts society's attitude unquestioningly.

56   *when she got confirmed* — baptized members of a Protestant church undergo a rite of confirmation, usually during adolescence, which strengthens their commitment to their faith and enables them to partake of Holy Communion, the bread and wine which represents the body and blood of Christ.

57   *Neapolitan* — of Naples in southern Italy.

57   *Capri* — an island off the Italian coast.

60   *Shows her a bundle of papers* — Helmer likes to impress Nora with the amount of work he has to do, which seems to increase his importance.

60   *If little squirrel asked you really prettily* — Nora decides to exploit her role as the pampered pet.

61   *But you can get rid of one of the other clerks instead of Krogstad* — Nora's only concern is to solve her own particular problem. She has no consideration whatsoever for anybody else, especially if she does not know them personally.

61   *I really believe it would have lost him his job* — presumably Helmer performed some kind of 'cover-up' operation?

61   *Your father was not a man of unassailable reputation* — by helping him conceal his misdemeanours, neither was Helmer. But, having regained a position of social esteem, he is not about to let it go.

62   *Do you expect me to make a laughing-stock of myself* —
Helmer's preoccupation is always with his own image in society.

62   *I am man enough . . . We shall share it . . . There, there,
there; don't look at me with those frightened little eyes* — his
paternalistic attitude is crucial to their relationship. At this point
they both believe in his ability to 'do the manly thing'.

65   *asparagus* — a vegetable regarded as a luxury.

65   *foie gras* — very expensive pâté.

65   *truffles* — edible fungi considered a delicacy.

68   *The maid enters with the lamp* — the lamp dispels the gloom.
Nora self-consciously uses the lamp as a symbol when she chides
Rank for his behaviour.

70   *He is wearing an overcoat, heavy boots and a fur cap* — his
appearance is made more threatening since his attire increases his
physical bulk. He brings the threat of the outside world into Nora's
protected, artificial environment.

71   *duns* — those who repeatedly press for repayment of debt.

71   *hack journalists* — abbreviation of 'hackneyed', therefore
journalists who write trite, commonplace articles without
imagination or insight.

75   *Here's his card* — his visiting card.

75   *Now, now, don't get alarmed* — Helmer never takes Nora's
reactions seriously until it is too late. He treats her like a child
whose game has been interrupted.

75   *And your husband has the key?* — another example of
Helmer's control of the household.

76   *Goes towards the hall door . . . He moves towards the door
. . . at the door, turns* — Ibsen plays with the audience by
engineering Helmer's movements across several lines of dialogue so
that the greatest amount of tension is generated.

77   *You've forgotten everything I taught you* — an unconsciously
prophetic statement. Nora will decide to reject what he has taught
her about life and, specifically, about marriage.

78   *You must show me every step of the way. Right to the end
of the dance* — She is pleading for Helmer's help in the Dance of
Life. Nora consciously imbues her own statements with
significance as she views herself as the central character in a tragedy.

78   *My child shall have her way* — as Helmer's paternalism
becomes even more pronounced, it sounds increasingly
inappropriate.

Act Three

84 *You'll catch cold if you stay out here* — Helmer's statement acquires significance in retrospect when Nora chooses to go 'out there' for good.

86 *I say that really was a magnificent champagne* — Helmer is slightly drunk, hence his embroidery and knitting demonstrations.

87 *I hope you'll manage to get home all right* — the nineteenth-century gentleman's chivalry deserts Helmer in his anxiety to be alone with Nora.

87 *Soon I shall sleep* — a self-consciously significant remark — Nora is thinking of her intended suicide.

87 *just like a real big human being* — Helmer's attitude is becoming suffocatingly unbearable. Ibsen loads the audience's sympathy towards Nora.

87 *my most treasured possession* — the clearest declaration of ownership; nineteenth-century women usually had no financial or political autonomy. They were indeed 'owned' by men, either their fathers or husbands.

90 *At the next masquerade, I shall be invisible* — like Nora, Rank indulges in self-consciously significant remarks.

91 *Here's a broken hairpin* — Nora has been trying to pick the lock.

91 *Then it must have been the children* — even at this point she tells a silly lie.

91 *Two visiting cards* — one would surely have been sufficient; the fact that Rank leaves two underlines his self-dramatising tendencies.

92 *so that I could offer my life and my blood* — the pose and language of a hero in melodrama

93 *I am in the power of a man who is completely without scruples* — now Helmer experiences something of how Nora has felt.

94 *This thing must be hushed up* — just as Nora's father's misdemeanours had been? Helmer's terror of social rejection is clear. His solution is always the same.

94 *Nora does not move* — her stillness is all the more remarkable after her restlessness and frantic dancing.

94 *The maid is standing half-dressed in the hall* — the servants have no right to a life of their own. The upsets amongst their superiors cause them great inconvenience which is not even remarked upon.

95 *I am saved! . . . You too, of course* — the afterthought underlines his total egocentricity.

95   *your feminine helplessness* — although this sounds crass at this point, it should be remembered that this is precisely the quality that Nora has sought to exploit earlier in the play.

96   *she has become his property in a double sense . . . not only his wife but also his child* — the most explicit statement of the typical nineteenth-century husband's sense of ownership.

97   *Sit down there, Torvald* — Nora now bosses him around in just the same tone he normally reserves for her.

103   *The servants know about everything to do with the house — much better than I do* — Nora acknowledges what the audience has observed to be the truth.

Above: Rank, Torvald and Nora. *Opposite and overleaf*: four phases of the relationship between Nora and Torvald

Questions for Further Study

1. How indebted is *A Doll's House* to popular nineteenth-century forms such as the well-made play and melodrama?
2. Is *A Doll's House* a naturalist or a symbolist drama?
3. Ibsen stressed that the play was about human, rather than women's, liberation. To what extent does the play bear this out?
4. Consider the part played by money in *A Doll's House*.
5. What does *A Doll's House* tell us about Ibsen's attitude to 'bourgeois morality'?
6. What is the relationship between 'truth' and 'illusion' in *A Doll's House*?
7. Consider the implications of role-playing in *A Doll's House*, especially as it affects concepts of gender.
8. What part do 'the past' and 'inheritance' play in *A Doll's House*?
9. 'The issues are so serious that Ibsen the humorist tends to be overlooked, as is the fact that *A Doll's House* is actually a serio-comic play; even the final scene has its comic aspects.' To what extent is *A Doll's House* a comedy, a serious drama, or a mixture of both?
10. How significant are the roles of Dr Rank and Mrs Linde within the overall scheme of *A Doll's House*?
11. How significant is the role of the children and servants in *A Doll's House*?
12. In what ways does the play prepare us for Nora's 'conversion' at the end of *A Doll's House* and does the process seem to you to be both logical and convincing?
13. In what ways does Ibsen use stage lighting, costume and properties in *A Doll's House*?
14. How important is stage movement in *A Doll's House*, especially exits and entrances and the function of stage doors?
15. What is the significance of animal and bird imagery in *A Doll's House*?

16. How is the external world of nature represented in *A Doll's House* and in what ways does it impinge on our understanding of the play?

17. Consider the role played by 'society' in determining private and public behaviour in *A Doll's House*.

18. What is the significance of music, song and dance in *A Doll's House*?

19. Analyse the different ways in which Nora relates to the men in her life, both living and dead.

20. What part does 'deception' play in *A Doll's House*?

21. Why does Ibsen call the play *A Doll's House*? Would a more accurate title be *A Dolls' House*?

22. Ibsen is on record as describing Mrs Alving in *Ghosts* as a version of Nora in later life. What light does a reading *of Ghosts* and the character of Mrs Alving shed on how we might interpret *A Doll's House* and the role of Nora?